THE ULTIMATE RETIREMENT GUIDE FOR 50+

ALSO BY SUZE ORMAN

You've Earned It, Don't Lose It

The 9 Steps to Financial Freedom

The Courage to Be Rich

The Road to Wealth

The Laws of Money, The Lessons of Life

The Money Book for the Young, Fabulous & Broke

Women & Money

Suze Orman's 2009 Action Plan

Suze Orman's Action Plan

The Money Class

The Adventures of Billy & Penny

Suze Orman's Will & Trust Kit

Suze Orman's Personal Finance Course

Suze Orman's 9 Steps to Financial Independence Online Course

THE
ULTIMATE
RETIREMENT
GUIDE FOR 50+

Winning Strategies to Make
Your Money Last a Lifetime

SUZE ORMAN

HAY
HOUSE

HAY HOUSE, INC.
Carlsbad, California • New York City
London • Sydney • New Delhi

Published in the United States by: Hay House, Inc.: www.hayhouse
.com® • *Published in Australia by:* Hay House Australia Pty. Ltd.: www
.hayhouse.com.au • *Published in the United Kingdom by:* Hay House
UK, Ltd.: www.hayhouse.co.uk • *Published in India by:* Hay House Pub-
lishers India: www.hayhouse.co.in

Indexer: Joan Shapiro
Cover design: Aaron Robertson
Interior design: Julie Davison

Cataloging-in-Publication Data is on file
at the Library of Congress

Hardcover ISBN: 978-1-4019-5992-0
E-book ISBN: 978-1-4019-5993-7
Audiobook ISBN: 978-1-4019-5994-4
Autographed edition ISBN: 978-1-4019-6049-0

12 11 10 9 8 7 6 5 4 3
1st edition, March 2020

Printed in the United States of America

This book is dedicated to Carla Fried.

*For the past 15 years, every book, blog, and article
I have published has been a true collaborative
effort between myself and the brilliant Carla. It is
not very often that a working relationship between
two people lasts as long as ours has. But if I were to
look back over the greatest gifts that I have ever been
given, I would so put Carla near the top of that list.*

*Carla, I thank you for all you have given
to this work. I know our words have truly made
this world a better place for all. Thank you
from the bottom of my heart.*

READER'S NOTE

It is my hope and suggestion that you will read every single page of this vital book. However, I also know that many of you will go directly to the chapter that best relates to your current financial situation.

I have made it easy for you to do just that: If you have not yet retired, Chapter 3's "Making the Most of Your Working Years" will answer the majority of your questions. If you are already in your 70s, most likely you will skip Chapter 5's "Power Moves for Your 60s." If you are just about to begin taking your Required Minimum Distributions, beefing up on Chapter 7 ("How and Where to Invest") will make the most sense as you map out your investment strategy. However you choose to read this book, know that each chapter is a complete unit unto itself.

Also, as we were going to press, a bill with far-reaching impacts on retirement plans was signed into law. This bill is known as the SECURE Act. We have done our best in this book to cover the legal changes that will most likely affect you in your retirement years. But you can also visit my website, suzeorman.com/retirement, for the most up-to-date information about the SECURE Act.

Just know that I want you to use this book for the rest of your life. I have filled it with information to help you in every stage of your retirement and written it with clear and concise guidance on every page.

I know it will guide you to your Ultimate Retirement years, so please enjoy reading it as much I enjoyed writing it.

CONTENTS

CHAPTER 1

YOUR ULTIMATE RETIREMENT STARTS HERE

When I first started my career as a financial advisor, 40 years ago, I knew right away that I would specialize in retirement planning. I had a kinship with clients who walked into my office full of fear and anxiety as they neared retirement. They knew they had some seriously consequential decisions to make—ones that would affect their quality of life in retirement—and they were wary of placing their future in the hands of an outsider who couldn't possibly know what kept them awake at night and what mattered most to them, and who likely couldn't relate to the momentous life change they were facing.

Well, they were right about the last thing—I was just at the beginning of my career and had no intention of slowing down anytime soon. But I could absolutely relate to the trepidation and vulnerability they felt about placing their lifetime savings in the hands of a stranger. Why? Because I had been taken advantage of by a broker earlier in my adult life, when I was working as a waitress. I had a $40,000 loan from customers and friends that was meant to help me start my own restaurant. I entrusted that vast sum to a hotshot young broker who put it all in a high-risk investment product without warning me of the potential downside. And guess what? I lost it all. It was devastating to me; it wasn't even my money to lose! It felt like the end of my dream—but it also ignited the fire in me to become a financial advisor who would earn the trust of her clients. It became my mission to help people on the verge of retirement keep their earnings safe and secure.

As I write this today, I am 68 years old. There's no question anymore about whether I can relate to people nearing retirement, because I too have decades of my working life behind me. The time in the future when I will no longer work is not all that far away. I have plenty of expertise in the psychological and emotional tugs that take hold as we age, and I have empathy in spades—for your hopes, your fears, and your wishes for the generations ahead of you and the loved ones in step beside you. The advice I have to share in this book comes from a heart that knows money decisions are never just about money. And I have an appreciation that what you must figure out is far more complicated than what my clients and I had to contend with back in the 1980s.

Back then, for those who didn't want stock market risk in their portfolio, I would recommend 30-year Treasury bonds that paid up to 15.5% interest. I have to tell you, it was one of the best investments I ever made for my clients. Money market accounts were paying more than 18% interest, so it was easy to park money there while you came up with an investment strategy. Inflation was high as well, but not as high as the yields my clients could earn on safe savings. If they worried about the volatility of stocks—there were three bear markets between 1968 and 1982—they could just stick with their safe income investments.

Perhaps the biggest difference was that back then the 401(k) and defined-contribution plans had yet to upend retirement planning. Most people did not have to decide what to do with large lump sums of money. Most of my clients were retiring from a company where they'd worked for 30 years or more. And that meant they were retiring with solid pensions that reflected a lifetime of service. The guaranteed monthly income from their pension (and for many, Social Security income too) provided enough to live on comfortably. Moreover, most companies offered retirees health care benefits to supplement Medicare. Today, very few do. It really was a simpler time back then. People did not fear retirement. They looked forward to it.

Today it's a whole different story. Most companies stopped offering pensions long ago; today it's only common for public-sector workers to have a pension. And even those who are fortunate enough to have a pension fear that it will be underfunded.

Most people have had to fund their own retirement by saving their money in 401(k)s and IRAs. Now they must make decisions about how to manage the money they have saved. They wonder whether they should just leave their money in their former employer's plan or move it elsewhere. If they move the funds, how should they invest them?

The most stressful decision for many people is deciding how much can be withdrawn each year. Taking out too much money in the early years of retirement raises the risk that there will be no money left for those who live into their 90s. And living into your 90s is no longer an outlier event; it's now quite common.

Taxes are another challenge; most people who are in their 60s today have saved for retirement in accounts where every dollar they withdraw in retirement will be taxed as income.

For some time now, interest rates have been virtually nonexistent—good luck finding a safe, nonfluctuating investment that will offer you more than 2.3% interest. Some good news is that inflation has been even lower than the interest rates paid on safe savings, but today's low yields make it hard to imagine living solely off the income from safe investments, as your parents and grandparents did.

What about Social Security? Will it be there for you when you retire?

And what about volatility in the stock market? Though the market (as of the writing of this book) is at an all-time high, there are indications that we are heading toward a recessionary time. Is the market safe enough for your money at this stage of your life?

There are for sure a lot of challenges today: so many unknowns that loom on the near horizon for those of us within a decade or two of retiring and those who have settled into a retirement that may last for two or three decades. That is what compelled me to write this book.

I have always believed in that time-tested adage "Where there's a will there's a way." You are here with me now, reading these pages, because you have *the will* to confront this situation head-on, armed with information that will build your confidence. *I will show you the way.* In the chapters ahead, I will guide you toward making decisions that will deliver you to your ultimate retirement.

CALLING ALL WARRIORS

I have news for you: The most valuable asset you own at this stage of your life is your spirit. It's not your retirement money, not the equity in your home, but the attitude and energy you bring to the job of planning your future.

How you think about yourself today and how you envision your future are everything. A positive, can-do attitude will carry you forward into the future when times are good but also when times are not so good. If you're able to face the future with the strength and conviction that you can handle whatever comes your way, well, your future will indeed be bright. And that's the goal, right? Being able to face the future without fear, being able to envision better things ahead—that is what makes the so-called golden years truly golden.

But sadly, that's not what I'm hearing from many of you. When you talk to me about your impending retirement, I have to tell you, your attitude is not all that positive! You tell me you're worried that you won't *be able* to retire. You tell me you are so angry/frustrated/embarrassed that you didn't do more or do better with your money when you were younger. You tell me you're worried that everything you've done up to this point—saving diligently, living within your means—will not be enough. I hear from many of you who are retired now and yet are still worried you haven't done enough or done it right.

Please listen closely. Stop focusing on what you didn't do or could have done differently. Stop beating yourself up about how you should have more, or how you should be in control of your finances at this point in your life. Stop being paralyzed by the fear of what may happen years from now.

I have a firm belief when it comes to money: Fear, shame, and anger are the main obstacles to wealth. They push us to do the wrong things and miss out on the smart choices that can move us toward our financial goals.

I am asking you to let go of any fear, shame, or anger that lurks around retirement planning issues.

You can't rewrite history, undo the past, or predict the future. But in terms of your money, you do have total control over how you will live right here, right now. There is so much you can do—and must do—before you actually retire that will help you realize the life you want to live in retirement. For those of you who are already retired, there is always the opportunity to reconsider and refocus your plan to make it work even better for the years ahead. I wrote this book for you: the worried, the fearful, the anxious. I know you need help navigating the road ahead. I've steered people toward happy and secure retirements my whole life, and now it's your turn. I titled this book *The Ultimate Retirement Guide* because I have plenty of advice to share. I haven't left anything on the table. In this book, I'm putting it all out there. Strategies. Dos. Don'ts. Challenges. But honestly, none of that really matters if you can't master this one essential requirement:

The only way to conquer fear is through action.

Your optimism and resolve will be what transforms the advice in these pages into actions and decisions that will propel you and your family toward the future you deserve. That means no focusing on the rearview mirror of life. Look at what you have today and what you can do to create the tomorrows you want and deserve.

SUZE'S STORY

A few years into my career, the retirement landscape began to change for some of my clients. In 1987 Pacific Gas and Electric, the utility company for Northern California, was offering employees an early retirement package. They had decided to lay off thousands of workers who were in their early 50s. This news was not something the workers had expected; they assumed, of course, that they had a good 10 to 15 years of solid employment ahead of them. What a shock, then, when they were told their time at the company was up. Most of the employees being laid off had been with the utility for 25 years or more.

PG&E hired me to give retirement seminars for their employees who had been offered early retirement. And here is what I learned from seeing hundreds of people who were suddenly out of work: Those who had an optimistic attitude, who believed they could make it work, would in fact make it work. Those who were afraid and angry, who believed PG&E had ruined their lives, had a hard time getting past those emotions and gaining control over their finances.

Their actual financial situation had little to do with it. There were executives who were retiring with a monthly pension of more than $10,000—this was more than 30 years ago!—and a few million dollars in savings. They were financially set, yet so many I met with were angry and focused on the past, not their future.

Then there were the workers who were being shown the door with a $2,000 monthly pension and had $200,000 or so in savings. They were of course jolted by their impending job loss, but their focus was on how to make it work. And they did make it work—by making smart decisions about their pensions, by sometimes finding new work, by spending less, and, in some instances, by making a physical move to a less expensive home, or a less expensive city, to save money. They focused on what they had and what they could have in the future.

For you to live the retirement you deserve, you need to let go of the past. Maybe there were some bad financial decisions at some point that derailed you. Maybe it was a divorce or an unexpected death. Maybe the Great Recession did a number on you or your loved ones, and you are still digging out financially. Maybe you are totally underwater paying back your kids' student loans. Maybe it's on you to take care of your aging parents. I get it—all these things, and plenty more, can sap your spirit as well as your finances.

But here is something I would like you to do every time you begin to feel anxious and afraid. I want you to look in the mirror and say these words:

I am a warrior, and I am not going to turn my back on the battlefield.

I am well aware that my critics will sink their teeth into that one. "Are you kidding me, Suze? *That's* the advice you're giving people?" To which I would reply, "Oh, you bet it is." For here is the scoop, my friends. If you cannot pick yourself up, if you cannot start taking action right now, then who is going to do it for you?

Look around you. Who cares about your money more than you do? The answer is no one. What happens to your money directly affects the quality of *your* life—not my life, not some financial advisor's life, but your life.

Why a warrior and why a battlefield? Why did I choose these words to bolster your spirit? Because I want you to know that you have the strength and you can summon the courage to move toward your goals no matter what is in front of you. And because I know it is not always easy.

You have the power within you. We all do. It's just a question of summoning the courage and the determination to tap that power. Together we can do this. Together we will tackle all the decisions that come into play at this stage of your life so that you can be free to actually enjoy your retirement.

The ultimate retirement as far as I am concerned is one in which you are not stressed about money. I don't want you to spend your retirement worrying whether your savings are going to last. I don't want you to spend your retirement nervous about whether you made the right choices with your investments. You deserve so much more than fear in your later years.

I can help you overcome all of that. No matter where you are in your financial life, no matter how much money you have or how little, you will find yourself in these pages. This book is not for your adult kids or grandkids. It is for anyone who is at least 50 years old and needs help laying out all the pieces of their retirement puzzle and then pulling them together into a cohesive plan. That includes those who are still working and want to keep working for many more years, as well as retirees eager to consider strategies that may increase their calm and confidence. There is always time and opportunity to adjust, adapt, and improve one's retirement strategy.

What awaits you in the pages ahead? In the next chapter, we talk about family, and how much—if at all—you can afford to provide financial support to your loved ones. Get perspective on that issue, and you will be in a far better position to create a secure retirement. Chapter 3 is for those of you who are still working; it is chock full of advice on moves to make (and to not make) between now and retirement. Then we need to have a clear-eyed chat about where you will live in retirement (Chapter 4). From there I have a mega checklist of decisions you need to make before you reach age 70 (Chapter 5). The next two chapters (6 and 7) tackle how to build a reliable stream of income that can last you 25 to 30 years and strategies for investing money in your retirement accounts.

If all of that makes your head spin, and you feel that you need more help, then by all means work with a financial advisor. In Chapter 8 I explain how to find a talented professional who will do right by you. Anyone can call themselves a financial advisor, yet many are nothing more than salespeople looking to earn a commission off selling you something. I won't let you fall into that trap.

Chapter 9 is, to be honest, my favorite of all—and if you have read any of my previous books or watched my public television specials, it won't come as a surprise to you. This chapter explores the must-have documents you can create today, and the decisions you can make today, that will remove stress from your life and your children's lives.

Yes, I am talking about wills and trusts and laying out your health care wishes. I can't overstate what a relief it will be to know you have everything in place. It frees you from so much worry in your retirement years. That is why I love it so much. This chapter is what will make it possible for you to relax. Knowing that you have done everything in your power to ensure smooth transitions is an incredible feeling.

There is for sure a lot to digest in the pages ahead. Many of the actions I propose will require some difficult conversations, both with yourself and with loved ones. I've always preached that courage is a necessary component of wealth—the courage to face the future, with all of its difficult decisions and inevitable challenges. In this book, I will minimize the unknowns wherever possible and bolster you to dig deep and find the warrior within. I want to help you arrive at a point where you can look toward the future with confidence and optimism. I hope you will dive in with the spirit that propelled me as I wrote the book: Making smart choices in your 50s and 60s will give you the gift of not having to worry about finances in your 70s, 80s, and 90s. And that is the ultimate as far as I am concerned.

So, are you ready, my fellow warriors? Turn the page and let's get to work.

CHAPTER 2

FAMILY TIES: HOW TO HELP THE ONES YOU LOVE WITHOUT HURTING YOUR RETIREMENT

The first step in building a secure retirement is to make sure that your heart is not making all the financial decisions.

And when it comes to your family, your heart is always, always, always engaged.

A parent never stops being a parent. Adult children are always and forever your "kids."

A parent who becomes a grandparent is blessed with the opportunity to love and nurture a new generation.

As precious and enriching as those relationships are, they can also become pressure points as you near retirement and once you are retired.

It is a very tough thing, I know, to step away from your decades-long role as provider. It is a fundamental, defining aspect of your identity. We all know that financial independence is an important milestone for an adult child that carries with it the confidence and strength to navigate one's way through life. Yet there is no clear playbook on when—and how—this should happen.

Sometimes it is necessary to provide support to an adult child. But often it is something that parents just keep doing, without giving careful thought to whether the financial support is helping a child build toward financial independence or inadvertently encouraging them to not make it a priority. We also do it without really thinking through the ramifications on our own finances in the long term.

While you may have been in a hurry to be on your own, your children may opt to stick around for a while. More adult children in their 20s and 30s live with their parents than did when you and I were their age. Living at home can be such a smart move for young adults who are juggling new careers that may not yet pay well, repaying student loans, and in no rush to dive into an expensive rental market.

What I don't think is healthy—emotionally or financially—is when that adult child living in your home doesn't contribute to household costs. This has nothing to do with tough love. This has everything to do with continuing to be the strong, supportive parent who helps guide your children to become their best selves.

That requires treating an adult child as an adult. If they live with you, they must contribute to the household costs. Asking them to participate as an adult is helping them become an adult.

Even if your kid isn't living with you, chances are you continue to help. Recent surveys report that many parents with adult children help those children with rent, groceries, car loans, student debt, and vacations. Sometimes into the 30s and beyond.

Parents say they are doing this with money they would otherwise—should otherwise—be directing into their retirement savings accounts. Their eyes are wide-open to the opportunity cost of providing continuing financial support. They are aware that they are potentially putting their future security at risk by continuing to support their adult children. Those parents are conscious of the fact that the money they spend on their adult children is money they really should be socking away for their future, yet they can't stop themselves from being the provider. To me, that is the saddest part of this unhealthy financial dynamic.

In this chapter I am going to share with you my perspective on the ways financially supporting adult children can hold both of you back. I am not going to tell you to stop contributing. Nor would I ever want you to abruptly change things, leaving your kids confused and in a financial lurch. However, what I want is for you to differentiate between financial assistance that helps with kids' needs versus money that funds their wants. And I will ask you to consider ways you can right-size your support so that it does not endanger your future.

Then there are the grandkids. Oh, the grandkids! Aren't they the best? You don't have to sweat all the tough things that go into raising them; you can just *revel* in them. But this relationship also needs a careful financial vetting. I know many of you see your children struggling to give your grandchildren a broad menu of experience and opportunity. Your provider gene kicks in, and you announce that you will help with the private school tuition, the after-school enrichment programs, the private coach, the summer camp, college tuition at your grandchild's dream school, or contributing to a 529 College Savings plan, regardless of whether it is a strong financial fit for your family.

Again, I am going to ask you to carefully consider whether you can afford to help in the ways you are. In the here and now, the answer will always seem to be *yes!* But your spending today must not imperil your ability to support yourself in your 90s. As we will discuss throughout this book, someone who is 65 today stands a very good chance of being alive in their tenth decade.

Complicating your retirement is that you may also need to provide for your own parents. Increasingly, adult children are helping support elderly parents. Some of you have already been launched into the experience of assisting an elderly parent in navigating their health care and shifting physical capabilities, and adapting to life after their spouse dies. Providing financial support is a wrenching development. You want to help. You need to help. And yet stepping in can imperil your own retirement security.

I am extremely sensitive to the desire and the perceived need to do whatever it takes to keep your parents in the home they love, with the help they now need, or make it possible for them to move to an assisted living situation. If you can afford to provide that assistance, I can think of no greater use of money than to support those who have supported you.

But this is possibly the biggest stand-in-your-truth moment you will face in retirement. Many of you will have to make expensive trade-offs to provide this support for your parents. If you have children, that means you are putting your kids at risk of having to do the same for you at some point. Dollars you spend today to support your parents—and jobs you leave to care for your parents—mean you will have fewer dollars for your later life. You may be fueling a vicious cycle that can play out for generations.

Perhaps with that perspective, you may find it easier to work with your parents—and your siblings—to keep them comfortable and safe in a way that does not destabilize you and future generations.

I hope you will take a deep breath and read what I have to say with an open mind, and take to heart the suggestions I have for how to juggle your beautifully intentioned desire to help, without hurting yourself.

What we will cover in this chapter:

THE MOVES TO MAKE TO HELP THE ONES YOU LOVE WITHOUT HURTING YOUR RETIREMENT

Your Kids and Grandkids:

- Build a healthy money relationship with adult children.

- Resist co-signing for loans.

- Help build a financially healthy environment for your grandchildren.

Your Parents:

- Carefully consider the true cost of becoming a full-time caregiver.

- Be paid for your caregiving.

- Set a spending limit.

YOUR KIDS AND GRANDKIDS

Wanting to provide financial support for adult children and grandchildren comes from an instinctive parental urge to help.

But what often gets lost in that decision is the calculation of whether helping your kids today will burden them in the future. A big problem is what I call the "it's only" syndrome. It's only $100 or $200 a month to help with the rent. It's only an extra $20 a month to keep paying for their cell plan. It's only $200 to help with the car payment or repaying their student loan debt. It's only $1,000 a year to help send the grandkids to camp.

I want you to add up all the ways, big and small, you continue to provide support to an adult child, plus the money you spent in the last year on grandchildren. I think you may be shocked to see how much "it's only" is costing you every year. In my experience, it can add up to thousands of dollars—many thousands if there are several kids and grandkids.

I am not going to tell you to cut off a child who is struggling to make rent. But helping with a loan for a new car, continuing to carry an adult child on your health insurance and cell phone plan just because, and kicking in money for vacations: that's a hard no, in my opinion. When these parents tell me they don't have money to save for retirement, you know what I say? *"Well, of course you don't!"*

Let's focus on the opportunity cost of helping your adult kids instead of helping yourself. Let's say you're providing $300 a month in various types of parental aid. If you instead saved that $300 a month for the next 10 years, assuming a 5% annualized return, that's going to grow to nearly $47,000!

Now ask yourself how scaling back that spending could keep you financially independent into your 90s. Is it the money you think you don't have for purchasing long-term care insurance? Is it the money that is keeping you from paying off your mortgage before you retire? Is it the money that can make it possible to delay Social Security until you are 70 so you can receive the highest possible payout? Is it the money that, if saved today, could help pay for at-home care down the line, rather than needing your family to step in, financially or as a caregiver?

I hope that viewing these questions from the perspective of future financial independence will motivate you to reconsider the type and magnitude of support you can provide for your family.

Build a healthy money relationship with adult children.

Home Rules

As I mentioned earlier, if an adult child lives with you, they should contribute to household expenses. How much is up to you. I want to be clear that this is not solely about helping you financially; it is about respecting a child as the adult they are.

I want your child to set up an automated monthly direct deposit from their checking account into yours. This is not something to be left to their best intentions. Nor do I want it to be a constant point of discussion—or contention—in your home.

As you progress through this book, you may often greet advice with a shrug and the thought "I can't afford to do that, Suze." Please circle back to this discussion we are having right now. I think for many of you, the money your adult child contributes will allow you to tackle all sorts of financial goals. Paying down credit card debt, bulking up your emergency savings, paying down the remaining mortgage.

But if you don't have any pressing financial needs, you might consider setting the money aside for your kid. It's up to you when you "return" the money to them. Maybe you use it to help them fund a Roth IRA each year. As long as they have earned income of their own, you can provide the dollars to contribute to a Roth IRA. Or when they are working on moving out, you've just helped them cover the security deposit or jump-start their emergency savings fund.

Rent

If you have credit card debt or are still paying off a mortgage near (or in) retirement, I don't think you have any business helping with a child's rent. That said, if you are intent on helping, I hope you will set the lowest possible contribution level. Helping a child rent a room in a shared apartment or house is one thing; bankrolling their own place because they don't want roommates is not your concern.

A Car

You are never to help a child buy a new car. And don't you ever support them leasing. If a child needs a car, they should be shopping for a used car that they can pay for with the shortest-term loan possible. The average new car loan payment in 2019 was more than $500 a month for nearly 70 months. That is financially insane for anyone, let alone an adult child who should be spending the least amount possible to free up money for other goals: moving out, paying down student loan debt within 10 years, starting an emergency savings fund, contributing to a Roth IRA.

Health Insurance

Children under the age of 26 are allowed to remain on a parent's health insurance plan. Given that employers are increasingly requiring employees to shoulder more of the monthly premium cost and cover a bigger chunk of any care, this may not be the best financial decision for you. At a minimum, if your child is working, they should cover their share of the premium.

But I encourage you to consider taking them off your plan. Even if your child doesn't qualify for coverage at their job, they can get coverage through the Affordable Care Act's health care exchange (www .healthcare.gov). The younger they are, the lower their premium cost, and someone who is just starting out professionally may qualify for a subsidy.

This can be a big money saver for single parents, as it will enable you to switch your coverage from family to individual, which means a lower premium and a lower annual deductible.

Student Loans

If you are nearing retirement and have any outstanding debts, you have no business helping a child pay back their student debt. Getting your own finances in order takes precedence.

Moreover, I think many of your children likely have a manageable amount of debt. They may not feel like it is manageable, and that's where you may be able to step in with some perspective. A rule of thumb is that if a new graduate's total loan balance is less than they will earn in their first year of work, they should be able to pay off the loan in 10 years. The average student loan balance these days is less than $40,000. That suggests that plenty of graduates will have enough income to handle the monthly payments on a 10-year standard repayment plan. If your children come to you asking for help repaying their college loans, I am asking you to discuss their overall spending before you agree to step in and help. Is their problem with the student loan because their rent and car payments are so high? Before you make the trade-off of helping them pay back student loans, I think it is reasonable to ask them to make the right trade-offs in their own spending.

What about helping pay for grad school? Absolutely not, unless you are completely sure it will not imperil your retirement security. No guessing or hoping allowed. This is where sitting down with a fee-only financial planner can help you carefully run the numbers. In Chapter 8 I explain how to shop for a reputable financial planner.

Resist co-signing for loans.

Being debt free in retirement will be a central driver of your financial and emotional security. That's the first reason why I don't want you to co-sign a loan for a child without serious consideration of what you are putting at stake.

You may think this is no big deal; you're just co-signing. It's not like you need to shell out money each month to pay back the car loan, student loan, personal loan, or mortgage. You know your kid, and you know there is no chance there will be any slipup.

You sure? I know your kid has every intention of staying on top of the payments. But what if he or she loses a job or becomes ill? You will be expected to step up and pay back the loan.

The other problem I have is that I think there can be a tendency for a child to borrow more—because they can—when a parent co-signs. I know that's not your fault, nor is it your intention, but co-signing is often the gateway to kids taking on more debt than they need, at the cost of not having more dollars to put toward important financial goals.

Help build a financially healthy environment for your grandchildren.

You have two relationships to navigate here: what your children may expect you to contribute toward grandchild-related expenses and your own personal money relationship with your grandchildren.

Let's start with your kids. By now you likely know what I am about to say: Just because you want to help your kids does not mean you can or should. This is the opposite of being selfish. Making sure you have enough money to take care of you is how you keep your kids—and maybe even your grandkids—from having to step in years from now.

I know this may seem difficult to ponder. It is not easy to disappoint anyone, let alone the people you love most. But again, you are focused on the here and now. If you look into your future, I think your kids will be so glad you carefully managed your finances.

I offer you some advice that has helped me navigate family relationships:

Say no out of love, rather than yes out of fear.

Your love for them is what motivates you to make difficult but loving choices that will protect them by keeping you financially independent.

It is my hope that you will also look for opportunities to provide some parental guidance on financial choices. I realize this can be treacherous. You don't want to tell an adult child what they should do. Saving for college is the area I am most concerned about. Young parents often make the mistake of saving for college the minute their child is born. Don't get me wrong: That is a wonderful instinct. But it is nonetheless the wrong move if they have credit card debt, don't have an eight-month emergency fund, and aren't saving 15% of their salary in retirement accounts. All of those priorities take precedence. If your kids ask you to contribute to their college savings plans for your grandkids, I would love for you to step in and ask how they are doing on those other important financial goals. Tell them Suze says she wants the best for those grandkids, and she says saving for college is not the family's top financial priority. There are loans for college—and plenty of ways to get a college degree with a moderate amount of debt. There are no loans for retirement.

Now let's talk about your grandkids. And the gift giving. For starters, as your grandchildren age, my advice is to give shared experiences as gifts, rather than another toy, gadget, or gift card. Studies show that gifting an experience delivers more happiness than gifting stuff. Sharing a ball game, a movie, a trip to the theater, a hike, a fishing trip, a visit to the state fair or an amusement park is not just fun in the moment—it makes lasting shared memories.

If you want to give grandchildren money as gifts, I would talk to their parents first about how you hope the money is used. It is my belief that every child should learn from the earliest possible age the three-bucket approach: Spend, Save, Share. Every child should have the freedom to spend a portion of a cash gift on anything they want, with no judgment from the parents or grandparents. A portion should be saved. And every child should be encouraged to share a portion of their financial gifts with others. Instilling charity as a part of their life from a very young age is in itself a priceless gift.

Discuss your thoughts about the Spend, Save, Share approach with your kids before giving any money to your grandkids. Yes, it is your money, but you are not the parent here; they are. It is so important to respect that. Ideally, your kids already have a plan like this in place. If not, ask them their thoughts on what you propose. I am confident you can work out a system that makes everyone happy.

YOUR PARENTS

Carefully consider the true cost of becoming a full-time caregiver.

Millions of adult children in their 50s and 60s are now caregivers to their elderly parents. Many of those children—and it is typically the daughters—end up leaving their jobs to step in and provide full-time care.

If you—and your siblings—are ever contemplating having one of you provide this support, please first think through the financial cost. The loss of salary is obvious. If you are single, there may be the cost of health insurance, which if you are not yet Medicare-eligible (age 65) can mean a premium of hundreds of dollars a month, plus higher deductibles and co-pays than you may have encountered when you were covered through work.

Then there is the lost opportunity to keep saving for your retirement, and perhaps the matching contribution you are no longer getting from an employer. Quitting your job will also reduce your Social Security benefit, as you are no longer earning work credits.

If you are married, relying on one salary in your 50s and 60s could be risky, as there is no guarantee that the salaried spouse will not run into a layoff or illness.

Are all of those reasons not to become a full-time caregiver? Of course not. I respect that the decision may not be driven by the financial fallout. But I am asking you to at least understand the ramifications of this decision and consider whether there might be alternatives that don't put you at such risk.

I know that many of you are dealing with a parent who wants to stay in their home. But would selling the home and moving to a less expensive home or apartment leave enough profit from the sale to pay for the care your parent needs? Or pay for them to move to assisted living? If the answers to those questions are yes, then you need to start this conversation with your parent. These are options that allow you to keep working.

Or, as we will discuss in Chapter 4, would it be at all practical for a parent to come live with you? I know this is not logistically or emotionally feasible for all families. But for some it can be a wonderful solution that works on many levels.

Be paid for your caregiving.

If you do decide to become a full-time caregiver, you should be paid, if that is possible. Don't start with me that you are doing this out of love. Of course you are. It's also work that should be compensated.

A parent can pay the caregiving child. Or if there are siblings, those who aren't the caregiver should help out financially. Everyone can give relative to their situation. I am not naive; I know this subject is a powder keg for some families. I would still encourage you to make it clear what your expectations are. That's in your control. Hopefully you have solid relationships, and this is something your siblings will want to do. If not, you have tried.

If you or another family member is going to step in as a full-time caregiver, I suggest working with an elder law attorney to help draft a Personal Care Agreement. This is a legal document that spells out who will be responsible for paying the caregiver. I think it is a smart way for families to spell out how the child/sibling who is stepping in as the primary caregiver will be compensated. You can learn more at caregiver.org (www.caregiver.org/personal-care-agreements). You can search for elder care lawyers in your area at the website of the National Academy of Elder Law Attorneys (www.naela.org/Web/Consumers_Tab /Consumer _Resources/Find_Lawyer.aspx).

The Personal Care Agreement should also spell out that the child or sibling who will be the primary caregiver has a certain number of free hours each week. This is non-negotiable—do you hear me? Caregivers must be given the space to be their own person, whether that means vegging out in the backyard, meeting friends for a movie or dinner, taking a walk in the park or an exercise class. And you'd better believe that contract needs to spell out at least two weeks of vacation, when someone else will step in to give the caregiver time off.

How much your family should pay the child/sibling who steps in as the caregiver is going to depend on resources. If you are moving in with a parent (or they are moving in with you), that impacts everyone's finances. At a minimum, your family should cover the health insurance premiums for the caregiver, and be ready to step in with help on deductibles and co-pays. On top of that, there is to be a monthly salary. I want the salary to be enough that the caregiver will be able to contribute $7,000 a year to a Roth IRA. That's the 2020 maximum for anyone who is at least 50 years old.

REVERSE MORTGAGE TO PAY FOR CAREGIVING

If your parent owns their home outright and is determined not to move, a reverse mortgage could provide the income they (you!) need in order to provide assistance at home.

Please review my explanation in Chapter 4 of how reverse mortgages work. If you think this is something your family should consider, I am going to insist that you work with a financial planner to help you walk through all the trade-offs. In certain circumstances, a reverse mortgage line of credit can be a smart way to bridge an income gap for your parent, and in the process not burden you with having to provide financial support or stop working. That said, you need to be very sure you understand how they work, and what happens if your parent ultimately must move out of that home.

In Chapter 8 I have advice on how to find a reputable financial planner.

Set a spending limit.

Many adult children provide financial support to elderly parents. It is virtually instinctive: They took care of you; now it is your time to take care of them.

I understand that instinct. It is a loving instinct. But it may be unkind. To you. Some of you may be familiar with one of my guiding principles: For an act to be truly generous, it must be generous for both the recipient and the giver. When you use your savings and your retirement funds to support a parent, or it keeps you from contributing to your retirement accounts, you are treading on being ungenerous to yourself. As I explained earlier in this chapter, that then imperils your own kids. If you deplete your savings now, it raises the chance that your kids may need to step in and help you at some point.

I know what you're about to say: "Suze, I don't have a choice." Maybe you don't. But before you go there, I want you to dig deep and think through the alternatives. Starting with moving your parent to a less expensive housing situation. I know they want to stay in their home. I know how desperately you want to make that happen. But at what cost?

If you are still working, please don't slow down on your retirement contributions. If you are providing any financial support to an adult child, I want you to curtail that support if it means you will be able to support elderly parents and still stay on track with your financial goals.

Your kids can work. They can make different spending choices in their lives. They have the power to cope and adjust. Your parents don't.

I wish with every cell in my body that you had the money to do both. But my job is to help you stand in the truth of how to help without hurting. Scaling back support for an able adult child is the right move if you need those dollars to help an elderly parent.

LET TRUE GENEROSITY
BE YOUR GUIDE

I want to reiterate that I understand how natural it is to want to help your loved ones. For many of you, your ability to provide is enmeshed with your identity. I get it.

I am asking you to reconsider and potentially recalibrate your giving. As I shared, a gift must be as generous for the giver as it is for the recipient. If your financial assistance is making it less likely you will reach your retirement goals, that is not my definition of being generous.

I am asking you to keep this possibility front and center as you proceed through this book. There will be times where you may find yourself thinking you don't have the money to do what I am recommending. When you come to one of those moments, consider how right-sizing your family support could give you the flexibility to create a secure retirement. I can't imagine your family would be anything but thrilled that you are taking care of you. After all, it reduces the likelihood that you will need to lean on your own kids or grandkids.

YOUR ULTIMATE RETIREMENT CHECKLIST

❑ Calculate all the different ways you provide financial support to adult children, grandchildren, and parents. Note whether the help is for a need or a want.

❑ List your personal financial goals that you wish you had more money to devote to.

❑ Consider how reducing your support for others will enable you to achieve your ultimate retirement goals: security and not needing your family to support you later on.

❑ Say no out of love, not yes out of fear.

❑ Make sure you are helping your adult child become financially independent.

❑ Consider caregiving options for elderly parents that do not imperil your own retirement security.

CHAPTER 3

MAKING THE MOST OF YOUR WORKING YEARS

If you are still working, you are in a great position to improve your retirement picture because you still have an income to put toward a variety of goals.

For many of you, saving more is a top priority, yet you are struggling to come up with the extra dollars you wish you could be saving.

The solution, my warrior friend, is really quite easy. *Stop* spending so much. Don't you "Oh, Suze" me. In this chapter I am going to expose all the ways you are spending more than you need to. I do it with love, and with the hope that you will be excited to consider how changing your spending can give you the money you need to polish up some of your retirement goals.

While you may be focused on the need to save more for retirement, I am most concerned that you pay off all your debts before you retire. In Chapter 4 I have a detailed explanation of why I want you to pay off your mortgage before you retire if you intend to stay in your home. But I know for many of you there is also credit card debt lurking, and car payments. That has got to go. Carrying debt into retirement will make it impossible to live the ultimate retirement. How can you relax and enjoy yourself if you must spend a chunk of your retirement income each month to make expensive debt payments? In this chapter we are going to explore how to live below your means but within your needs. Does that sound like punishment? You couldn't be more wrong.

Not only will living within your means leave you with more money to put toward your financial goals, but it will also make your life easier in retirement. If you reduce your monthly spending by $500 or $1,000 a month today, that's $500 or $1,000 a month you won't need to generate in retirement. Spending less today reduces your retirement overhead. Not exactly punishment, when you think about the long-term payoff, right?

Your remaining working years are also a time when you can explore some smart retirement options. I know many of you have no plans to stop working. I think that's a great strategy; I am all for working until at least 70. But it also comes with risks that you need to plan for today. Starting with the fact that management may not share your enthusiasm for your continuing to work at your current job. And for those of you in your 50s (and 60s) and in good health, I want you to give serious consideration to whether a long-term care insurance policy makes sense for you. Even with rising premiums, once you do the math, they can still be a cost-effective way to protect yourself and your loved ones from the possibility of needing to spend large sums of money on your later-life care.

THE MOVES TO MAKE DURING YOUR WORKING YEARS

- Prioritize paying off all debt before you retire.
- Embrace living below your means.
- Save more for retirement . . . in the right accounts.
- Have a plan to work longer.
- Consider long-term care insurance.

Prioritize paying off all debt before you retire.

When I ask people what would make them feel financially secure, 9 times out of 10 the answer is being debt free. I couldn't agree more. Especially in retirement. If you still have a mortgage, and are carrying high-rate credit card debt and maybe a car loan (or two), you are putting a lot of pressure on your finances to be able to pay all those bills and still have plenty to cover your other needs—and let's hope plenty of wants too!

I bet you're a bit skeptical that you can pull this off. It's not as if you haven't wanted to tackle your debts for a long time. But you just cannot seem to find a way to make it happen.

Remember what I said earlier about your mindset: Everything is possible if you believe in yourself. Before you start down the road of negative thoughts, slam on the brakes. You most definitely can tackle your debt if you are ready to summon your inner warrior and take a fresh look at your spending habits.

Embrace living below your means.

So how are you going to become debt free?

By adopting a mind-set where your goal is to live below your means but within your needs. If you are ready to be honest, you know that your spending sometimes veers off to fulfilling wants more than needs. For example, you need a car. But let me ask you a question: Did you actually need to spend what you did on that car? Or did you just give yourself permission to spend more for something you wanted instead of buying a less expensive option?

Are you receiving this as if I'm asking you to eat your least favorite vegetable? Well, I am going to ask you to change that mind-set. This approach is not something that should depress you, or feel like a burden. When you can get to the point where you live below your means, you are giving yourself a shot at financial freedom. You know what should excite you? The ability in retirement to have the money you need to live the life you want, rather than be weighed down by big, expensive debt payments. Are you with me?

SUZE'S STORY

My wife, KT, and I are blessed to have more money than we need. Do we spend money? You bet. But I have to tell you, one of the things that has been a special bond between us is that we both get more pleasure out of the money we save than the money we spend. We truly enjoy living below our means.

Some examples of how we manage to save money:

We had multiple landlines in our Florida home for business calls, faxing, and personal use. We ditched those lines and are doing just fine with our cell phones. Now we e-mail the business correspondence we used to fax. Annual savings: nearly $1,000.

We have one car. One. And we have had it for 10 years.

Our home and auto insurance are with the same insurance company. That saves us hundreds of dollars a year. Keeping our FICO scores very high also helps keep our auto premium lower.

We only shop online if they have free returns. That way if we need to return something, it doesn't cost us anything.

We use credit cards that give us cash back, and we keep track of when they have special offers. Then we use the card that pays us the most. We get back a lot of money in a year.

We never go into a grocery store without a shopping list of everything we need, and we stick to that list. It's just that simple. That way we never spend more money than we planned on spending. And KT always checks for coupons when we go into a store to see if anything on our list is on sale.

We don't spend money on buying gifts. We only give and receive handmade gifts with our family.

I share those money-saving moves from the Orman-Travis household as proof that this need not be painful or difficult. All those decisions were easy to make, and each one brought us pleasure. I bet you can do the same, and likely find even more ways to trim your household spending.

Not all spending cuts will be as easy as cutting the landline. But again, this is a challenge with a valuable payoff: retirement security. With that as your motivation, I ask you to take a fresh-eyed look at some of your major spending choices:

The Kids

For those of you who still have high schoolers at home, you should know that your child's college choice can make or break your retirement. If you are behind on retirement savings, the biggest favor you can do for your kid is not pay for college.

Yes, you read that correctly. You need to funnel every penny into retirement savings. You're going to have to believe me—your kids are going to be so grateful that you chose to focus on retirement. Okay, maybe they won't be so grateful at age 18. But 10, 15, 20 years down the road, when they are raising their own families, they are going to be so relieved if you don't need to rely on them for support in your retirement.

Please give this serious consideration. Retirement saving must take precedence over paying for college. That means no borrowing on your part, and only make contributions to a 529 College Savings Plan if it does not in any way limit your retirement savings.

You can work with your kids to focus on colleges that will be so eager to have them attend that the net price—after financial aid—will be low enough that your child can cover any shortfall with federal student loans. Federal student loans are affordable and safe.

And as we covered in the previous chapter, if you have adult kids, I want you to give some serious thought to whether your financial support is truly necessary, and what scaling it back could do for your retirement security.

The Car(s)

What's sitting in your driveway or garage could explain a lot of your retirement stress. The average monthly payment for a new car loan in late 2019 was more than $500, and the typical loan runs for nearly six years. Both are financially indefensible in my opinion if you are struggling to save for retirement.

If you need a car, your goal should be to spend the least amount you can for a reliable car. That means used, not new. Don't you dare start in about reliability. Cars today are built to last.

If you need to take out a loan, I want you to commit to a term that is no longer than 36 months. If you take out a loan that you need more than three years to repay, then you are buying a car you cannot afford. You may say, "But, Suze, the monthly cost is higher on a shorter loan, so I'm spending more each month!" The truth is that with a shorter loan, you are spending less in the long run. The faster you pay off this depreciating asset, the less you will pay in overall interest and the faster you will have more monthly cash flow to put toward other financial goals, starting with retirement savings.

A smart move is to purchase a car that is just a few years old; look for certified pre-owned deals (CPOs) at dealerships. The cost of a used car that is a few years old—and still in good shape, of course—can be 40% less than the same model brand spanking new. Then aim to drive that car for at least 10 more years. You are not to trade in your car every three or four years. Do you hear me? Your goal is to get your loan paid off ASAP and then have many years when you won't be making a car loan payment. Instead, you can take that money and use it to pay down any other debts or save more for retirement.

For instance, let's say you had a loan that cost you $525 a month. After you pay off the loan, you keep driving that car loan-free and invest the $525 a month in a retirement account. In six years you would have saved $44,000, assuming a 5% annualized return. Let that $44,000 keep growing for another 10 years, and you will have more than $70,000. That's your choice: an expensive car loan or building retirement savings.

And if you are tempted to lease, please listen to me: Do. Not. Lease. Many of you lease a car because the monthly costs are typically lower than the payments on a loan. It's a bit of auto-lender sleight of hand that can be tempting—and very costly in the long run. Leasing is a financial trap. The typical lease is for three years, and then when the lease is over, the car is handed back and another car is leased. That means you are never not making monthly car payments. When you have other financial goals—saving more for retirement, paying off your mortgage, reducing your credit card bills—there is no way you can financially justify leasing a car.

The Home

I don't have to tell you that your housing costs eat up a big chunk of your monthly cash flow. In Chapter 4 we will consider a variety of housing moves that can solidify your retirement plan. Right now my goal is to plant a seed: Could making a housing move transform your retirement outlook?

I know many of you want to stay in your home. It can be wrenching to consider a move if you have had roots in the same house for years, with all the memories that are tied to it. But I ask you to at least open your mind to contemplate a few realities.

Those memories are about the people you welcomed into your home and the experiences that took place within it. You can move and still have those memories to share with your loved ones.

Please know that I am not asking you to do something that I myself have not done. As we grew older, KT and I realized that it was time for us to downsize as well. I thought that once we sold our San Francisco home, we would miss it terribly, but I knew it was the best financial move to make, so we sold. To my surprise, we don't miss it at all. We don't miss the extra bills and the long-distance property management. We are loving our life on the East Coast.

If you are willing to entertain a downsize, I would then ask you to also consider making a move sooner rather than later, if that is practical. Moving to a less expensive home could set off a wonderful cascade of retirement savings: You may have gains from the sale that you can add to your savings. You will also likely reduce your monthly housing costs—the rent/ mortgage, property tax, insurance, maintenance, etc.— and that can enable you to add more to your retirement accounts.

Lowering your housing costs might also make it easier to downshift to different work later on that pays less but that you enjoy more. As I explain later, I think this may be an important ingredient to being able to work until you are 70.

Emotionally—and physically—a move when you are younger is going to be a lot less stressful than a move in your 70s or later.

I know this is a very big decision. All I ask is that you not dismiss it as an option. If you have an open mind and run the numbers, I think you may be pleasantly surprised at how a move can help you close any retirement gap.

Taking all this to heart can turn your future into one that you will love living.

Save more for retirement . . . in the right accounts.

While you are still working, you can make it a priority to save even more in your retirement account.

First, let's review what you could be saving in retirement accounts, and then let's talk about which retirement accounts might make the most sense at this stage of your life.

In 2020 anyone who is at least 50 years old can contribute $26,000 to a 401(k) or 403(b) plan. In addition to those workplace plans, you are eligible to save $7,000 in an Individual Retirement Account (IRA). (Those limits are adjusted to keep pace with inflation.) And of course, you can always save more in regular taxable accounts.

Anyone in their 50s or 60s today has most likely done the bulk of their retirement investing in a pretax traditional 401(k) or 403(b) or a pretax traditional IRA. (Please note that what I say about a 401(k) plan below also applies to a 403(b) as well as the Thrift Savings Plan for federal employees.)

When you retire and withdraw money from these traditional accounts, every dollar is taxed as ordinary income. Plus, if you were born on or before 6/30/49, you must make withdrawals by April 1 after the year you turn 70½, or 72 if you were born after 6/30/49. If you receive a pension, that income is taxable as well. A portion of your Social Security benefit may also be taxed.

Your taxable income may be so high that you will be required to pay a higher monthly Medicare Part B premium. In 2020 an individual with income above $87,000 and married couples filing a joint return with income above $174,000 paid a higher premium than the base monthly cost of $144.60 per person.

Now I am very aware that there is a popular argument that your tax rate will be lower in retirement, so you should try to avoid taxes now while you are working and not sweat it so much in retirement.

That may not be true for you.

For starters, as I just explained, the more saving you have done in traditional 401(k)s and traditional IRAs, the more you will be required to withdraw in retirement, whether you want to or not. Those withdrawals will be taxable income, which could mean you may not see a big drop in your retirement tax rate.

Moreover, it is important to recognize that right now individual income tax rates are near historic lows and the federal deficit is not. None of us knows what the future will bring in tax policy, but I don't think anyone should be surprised if tax rates eventually rise.

I have a rule I want you to follow:

Invest in the known versus the unknown.

The known is your tax bracket today. The unknown is your tax bracket in the future.

There is no way to know what tax brackets will be years from now when you will have to start making withdrawals.

That leads me to my core advice for those still working: I want you to save money today in retirement accounts that will allow you to make withdrawals in retirement without owing any income tax whatsoever.

This makes so much sense if you have spent decades saving money in traditional 401(k)s and/or IRAs. Adding tax-free accounts sooner rather than later will give you valuable tax flexibility in retirement.

Tax-free Retirement Accounts

There are three ways to save money today that you can then use without owing any tax in retirement:

- A Roth 401(k)

- A Roth IRA

- A Health Savings Account (HSA)

I want you to learn about all three, and then you can make an informed decision on whether any—or all—might make sense for you over the last stretch of your earning years.

Roth 401(k)

Back in the day, when you started saving for retirement, the Roth 401(k) did not exist. Your employer only offered a traditional 401(k). With a traditional 401(k), what you contribute each year lowers your tax bill— your contributions reduce your taxable income—but the deal is that you will owe income tax on the money you withdraw from your traditional 401(k). Since the government is eager to finally collect tax on that money, you must make Required Minimum Distributions (RMDs). If you were born on or before 6/30/49, you must make withdrawals by April 1 after the year you turn 70½, or 72 if you were born after 6/30/49.

Nearly 15 years ago, the government gave retirement plans the option of also offering a Roth 401(k). With a Roth 401(k), you don't get the up-front tax break on your contributions. Instead, your contributions are made with money that has already been taxed. The payoff comes in retirement: Money you withdraw from a Roth 401(k) is tax free. No income tax. No capital gains tax. No. Tax. Period. So what you see in your retirement account is exactly what you will get. That's a big deal.

Chances are in the year 2020, your employer now offers a Roth 401(k) option; it's been a slow process, but nearly 70% of large plans have a Roth. (If your plan doesn't, get some colleagues to join you and lobby for it to be added to your plan.)

The problem is that most people who can save in a Roth 401(k) don't. You might not even realize it's an option.

I recommend you check to see if your plan has a Roth 401(k) option. Everyone is eligible if the plan has a Roth option; there is no income limit. That said, a quirk of 401(k)s is that if your employer makes a matching contribution, your employer's match money will be deposited in a traditional 401(k), even if your contributions are going into a Roth account. Just something to be aware of.

Roth IRA

If you are at least 50 years old in 2020 and your modified adjusted gross income (MAGI) is less than $124,000 ($196,000 for married couples filing a joint tax return), you can contribute the maximum $7,000 to a Roth IRA. Single filers with income between $124,000 and $139,000 and joint filers with income between $196,000 and $206,000 can make smaller contributions. Above those upper limits, you can't contribute directly to a Roth IRA. That said, there is a workaround for high-income households called a *backdoor Roth IRA*. With a backdoor you make a contribution to a traditional IRA with the intention of immediately converting that money into a Roth IRA. There can be a tax bill involved with this move if you already have money saved in traditional IRAs. If you are interested in a backdoor Roth IRA, I highly recommend consulting with your tax pro first to make sure it is a wise move for you.

> *Learn more* about backdoor Roth IRAs at my website: suzeorman.com/retirement.

If you can contribute to a Roth IRA, it is a fantastic way to save. What you contribute can always be withdrawn—at any age—regardless of how long your money has been in the account and without incurring taxes or penalties. And once you are 59½ and you have had the account for at least five years, you can withdraw your earnings (in addition to your contributions) without owing tax or an early withdrawal penalty.

Unlike a traditional IRA, the government does not require you to make RMD withdrawals from a Roth IRA. The money can sit there and grow, and be passed to your heirs. Also, when a Roth IRA passes to your beneficiaries, they can make tax-free withdrawals too. That's a very big deal.

You can open a Roth IRA account at almost any financial institution, from credit unions to discount brokerages such as Fidelity Investments, Charles Schwab, TD Ameritrade, and Vanguard. All of these financial institutions have lineups of low- or no-fee index mutual funds or exchange-traded funds you can invest your Roth in. (More on how to invest for retirement in Chapter 7.)

Health Savings Account

Medicare, which you become eligible for at age 65, will pick up a lot of your health care spending costs in retirement, but not all of your costs. For most retirees, Medicare ends up covering about 70% of medical expenses. The other 30% comes out of your pocket, or additional insurance you pay for. The nonpartisan Kaiser Family Foundation reported that in 2016, the average out-of-pocket expense for Medicare recipients was nearly $5,500.

This is where a Health Savings Account (HSA) can be a big help in retirement. An HSA offers three tax breaks: You get to deduct your contribution on this year's tax bill, the money in your HSA grows without being taxed, and money you eventually withdraw to pay for qualified medical costs won't be taxed.

Money you contribute to your HSA—and your employer may kick in some money as well—can be used to pay your current out-of-pocket medical costs, yet there is no requirement that you must use the money in your HSA every year. Unlike other types of health savings accounts your employer may offer, such as a Flexible Savings Account (FSA), there is no "use it or lose it" rule with an HSA. Money you don't use this year can just stay in the account and keep growing, just like an IRA or 401(k). That makes the HSA a potentially powerful addition to your retirement savings.

Now that said, an HSA needs to be carefully considered. You are only allowed to have an HSA if you are enrolled in a high-deductible health plan (HDHP). Many employers now offer an HDHP, or if you buy your insurance directly through the health care exchange, there are HDHP options. One advantage of an HDHP is that your (share of) the monthly premium will typically be lower than other types of coverage.

But there are trade-offs that you need to understand, starting with what's clear in the policy name: There's a high deductible.

In 2020 an HDHP must have a deductible of at least $1,400 for individuals and $2,800 for family coverage in order for the participant to be eligible to contribute to an HSA.

Moreover, the maximum total annual out-of-pocket cost can't exceed $6,900 in 2020 for an individual and $13,800 for family coverage.

This is where I want you to be careful: It only makes sense to consider an HDHP/HSA as part of a retirement plan if you have the savings to easily cover the deductible and maximum out-of-pocket costs.

If you're able to cover current medical expenses from savings, here's how the HSA can be a great way to save for retirement:

In 2020 individuals can contribute $3,550 to their HSA account. If the HDHP covers other family members, the contribution limit is $7,100. And if you are at least 55, you can add another $1,000 to those limits.

What you contribute reduces your taxable income for the year. For example, if you make $100,000 and contribute $7,100 to an HSA, your taxable income will be $92,900.

As I mentioned, you can always tap your HSA to cover current medical costs. But if you are able to keep it growing untouched until you retire, it becomes a valuable way to keep your taxes under control.

Let's say you are single and save $3,550 a year in your HSA for the next 10 years, and earn 5%. (In reality, the limits will rise with inflation, so you will be able to save more.) That will give you around $46,000 to use for qualified medical expenses without any tax bill.

> *Learn more* about HSA qualified medical expenses at my website: suzeorman.com /retirement.

Now let's say you are retired and you have a bad year, with big out-of-pocket medical expenses of $15,000. If you pull money out of a traditional 401(k) or IRA to pay that bill, it will all count as taxable income for the year. To net the $15,000, you may need to withdraw at least $18,000 to $20,000, depending on your federal and state tax liability. But if you tap your HSA, you just need to withdraw $15,000, as there is no tax bill.

And there's a neat way to make a big withdrawal from an HSA in retirement even if you don't have big medical bills that year. If you save your health care bills today, you can make a tax-free withdrawal decades later based on these "old" medical bills. For instance, let's say you have $15,000 in old medical expenses you paid for out of pocket over the years, and you kept receipts for all those bills that you didn't use your HSA to reimburse you for. Now let's say that 15, 20, 30 years later, you could really use $15,000 in tax-free money. As long as you still have the old receipts, you can make the $15,000 withdrawal from your HSA based on those old receipts. An added bonus: This strategy allows you to use the money for anything without incurring any tax, because the withdrawal was based on those old qualified expenses.

Have a plan to work longer.

I know many of you dream of retiring around 65. However, I have to tell you: Retirement in your 60s isn't all it's cracked up to be. Sixty-five is the new 55. You're still young! You don't feel old—you still want to be useful and contribute to society. So why not just stay in the game longer?

Can you adjust your goal and plan to retire at 70 or later?

Yes, you read that right: I want you to plan on working until you are 70. Maybe not in a high-powered, mega-demanding position. But working at a job that brings in some income.

It's just this simple: The longer you work, the more time you have to let your retirement funds grow. The longer you have a paycheck coming in, the longer you have to pay off the mortgage on your home.

If you retire at 62, or before, and live into your 90s, you could spend as much time in retirement as you did working. That's a very long time to ask your savings to support you. If you work until 70, you will likely still have plenty of time to be a full-time retiree.

If you continue to bring in some income until you are 70, you will also make it easier to follow one of the most important—and lucrative—retirement income moves: waiting until you are 70 to begin collecting your Social Security retirement benefit.

In Chapter 5 I have a detailed explanation of why I believe delaying Social Security until age 70 is a fantastic financial decision most everyone should choose. Here's the teaser: A recent analysis by United Income estimates that the average household would collect an additional $111,000 if they claimed Social Security later, not earlier.

What does this have to do with those of you who are in your 50s and 60s? Plenty. You need to have a plan if you're going to wait to claim your benefit. Basically you need to make sure you can earn enough from age 62 to 70 to offset what you're not collecting from Social Security. In 2020 the average annual Social Security benefit is around $15,000. (You can use the Social Security benefit calculator to get an estimate of what you may qualify for: www.ssa.gov /benefits/retirement/estimator.html.)

There are steps you can take today to increase the likelihood that you might be able to keep working through your 60s.

Stay relevant at work.

A survey by the Transamerica Center for Retirement Studies reported that many people near retirement want to keep working longer. But in the same survey, a large percentage of those 50-something folks admitted they weren't doing everything they could to shine at work.

As I write this in late 2019, our economy is still growing at a solid pace. But recessions are part of the normal cycle. When the next one hits, employers will start to cut jobs. When you are older and just coasting, you become an easy target for a layoff.

I appreciate that there is no defense for ageism. But don't make it easy for your employer to fall into that trap. If you are a rock star at work, you likely won't be at the top of the layoff list.

Even if you are laid off, if you have stayed up to speed on developments in your field, and can work with the latest technology, you will find it that much easier to hunt for another job.

There are so many ways to keep up. Do you take advantage of every on-the-job training session offered? If you know you are rusty, enroll in an online class that you can work through on your own schedule. (Check out sites such as LinkedIn Learning, Udemy, and Coursera.) Prefer a real class setting? Look for classes at your local community college.

Plot your 60s career downshift.

If you want to plan to keep working full bore at the same job you have now through your 60s, that's fine by me. Just keep in mind what I said earlier: Coasting will not work.

I think for many of you, what you need—and want—in your 60s is work that brings in just enough income so you can delay starting your Social Security benefit and avoid making withdrawals from your retirement savings (or be able to make smaller withdrawals).

If you have already spent decades saving for retirement, your 60s may be a decade when you don't necessarily save more, but just find a way to not touch your savings for up to 10 more years.

If that is your situation, then you may be able to downshift to a less demanding job in your 60s, if that appeals to you. Maybe your current job offers a flextime option that allows you a little more freedom. Or maybe you could do consulting in your field, or perhaps you're eager to finally focus on a hobby that you would like to transform into an income-generating venture.

If that's your intention for your 60s, by 55 I want you to be giving serious consideration to how you will make this transition. You may need to take some classes or get some certification. Or spend weekends shadowing people in a job you think you might like to pursue. Or volunteering at a job you think you might like to segue into.

The point is that you don't want to suddenly wake up at 60, snap your fingers, and expect to make a fluid transition in a few weeks. This takes fore-thought, experimentation, and careful preparation. Not sure where to start? Check out the website of Kerry Hannon, who has written a dozen books on career transitions and great jobs for the 50-plus crowd (kerryhannon.com). She is also AARP's Jobs Expert.

Consider long-term care insurance.

One of the trickiest aspects of retirement planning is that it is not easy or natural to think about who you will be at 80, 85, 90, and beyond. I also doubt you spend much time thinking about your 20- and 30-year-old kids as 50- and 60-year-olds who may someday help you navigate your retirement.

In both instances, you can help yourself and your kids by considering how you will be able to cover the cost of care if at some point you need help manag-ing everyday basics such as eating, bathing, using the bathroom, and getting dressed. Even if you are able to stay in your home, you may find it necessary—and a huge help—to have daily care. Moreover, at some point assisted living may be a better fit for a later-life you.

Though I know it is not something you want to think about, when you are in your 50s is when you can take steps that will buy yourself and your chil-dren peace of mind if you eventually develop demen-tia, Alzheimer's, or another debilitating illness, such as a stroke, that will make it necessary for you to have support to keep you safe and content.

If your goal is to keep your family from needing to step in with physical or financial support, then you need to plan today for how you would be able to hire the care you may need. The median monthly cost for an at-home aide or a private bedroom in an assisted living facility is around $4,000. If you ever need to spend time in a nursing home, the median monthly cost for a semiprivate room was $7,500 in 2019 and more than $8,500 for a private room, according to a Genworth survey. That's more than $100,000 a year for a private room. And you know those costs are just going to keep rising over the years.

Medicare does not cover long-term care costs. If you move to assisted living, the cost of your room and meals will not covered by Medicare; only medical care will be paid for by Medicare. Neither does Medicare cover a long stay in a nursing home. In 2020, the first 20 days spent in a skilled nursing home are paid for by Medicare. For days 21 to 100, Medicare enrollees have a daily co-pay of $176. After day 100, Medicare patients—or their families—are responsible for 100% of nursing home costs.

Your 50s is the ideal time to come face-to-face with these realities and decide on a financial plan that will prepare you—and your family—if you need care down the line.

If you have done a knockout job of saving for retirement and are confident you can afford the potentially high cost of care, you may be a candidate to "self-insure." That just means you anticipate having the savings needed to cover potential long-term care costs.

Not sure how much is enough? This is where working with a financial planner can be useful. You can find planners who will work on a project basis for an hourly or flat fee. In Chapter 8 I explain when it may make sense to work with a pro, and how to find a reputable one.

But if the prospect of later-life care costs is giving you nightmares today, I want you to consider the value of buying a long-term care (LTC) insurance policy.

The Case for LTC Insurance

Many people who bought LTC insurance years ago have been subjected to sharp premium increases that in some cases more than doubled their annual cost.

So why would I recommend LTC insurance? Because if you can afford the premium today and then need extensive care later on, the benefits you will receive over just a year or two will likely be more than the total premiums you paid for 30 years.

Furthermore, it is unlikely anyone buying a policy today will encounter huge premium spikes. What happened to earlier LTC policyholders is that when LTC insurance was first offered, the insurance industry miscalculated the cost of actually making good on these policies and paying out benefits. The premiums were set way too low, in hindsight, to cover the actual costs the insurers faced years later. Another complication was that for the past 10 years, insurers—like you—have been unable to earn much interest on safe investments.

Just so you know, insurers can't simply decide to raise premiums. They must petition state insurance departments for permission and prove they have costs that far exceed their premium income. Over the past decade or so, many insurers have been granted the right to raise their LTC premiums. (And many insurers have stopped offering new LTC policies.)

I am very aware of the financial hardship many early buyers have faced when premiums were increased, but as I said, I don't think this is going to be a common occurrence for new policies. Insurers are now better at pricing policies right out of the gate.

The time to focus on this is in your 50s and 60s because as you age, a pre-existing health condition could be grounds to deny you coverage. And the longer you wait, the higher your premium will be.

Now let's talk about cost. Your cost will depend on a variety of factors, but a 55-year-old couple in good health can buy a lot of protection for an annual premium of about $5,000 or so these days. Let's say you can handle the $5,000 premium today and you pay it for 30 years. That's $150,000.

To be extra safe, let's assume there will be a premium increase. Let's say somewhere along the line there is a hike, and your total cost over 30 years is $200,000. (I am purposefully using a big increase to make a point. But to be clear: I do not anticipate policies sold today by top-rated insurers will need to impose such big hikes.) Even at today's prices for at-home, assisted living, or nursing home care, you might recoup $200,000 in premiums if you need care for just a few years. And we know that the cost of care will be even higher 20 and 30 years from now.

The Hybrid Option

A newer type of LTC policy combines life insurance or an annuity with LTC insurance. Hybrid LTC policies have become more popular than traditional LTC policies the past few years.

The main appeal of a hybrid policy is that if you don't use the policy for LTC, or you use just a small portion, your heirs will receive a death benefit when you die. That payout could be as much as the premium cost for the policy, and commonly more.

Another benefit is that hybrid LTC policies are often paid for with one big premium payment, or a series of payments over 10 years or so. That reduces the risk of being smacked with a premium increase, but as I noted, I think this is unlikely moving forward.

And you may find the health-screening process for a hybrid policy easier than for a traditional.

But there's a catch. A very expensive catch.

A hybrid policy costs a lot more than a traditional LTC policy. It can be double or triple the cost. That's the price you pay to be assured that you—actually, your heirs—get something out of the policy if you never use it for LTC expenses.

Personally, I would rather you consider a traditional LTC policy; it's the more cost-effective way to plan for potential costs.

> *Learn more* about key features to shop for in an LTC insurance policy at my website: suzeorman.com/retirement.

Once more, I want to stress that assessing your needs and determining how much you can comfortably afford are critical. The Got LTCi website (www .gotltci.com) is run by Phyllis Shelton. I rely on Phyllis for her long-term care insurance expertise. I also recommend you consider working with a reputable planner who can help you sort through your options. In Chapter 8 I have advice on how to find a good planner who can help you wrestle with the LTC decision.

HOW TO HANDLE A PREMIUM HIKE FOR THOSE WHO ALREADY OWN AN LTC POLICY

For those of you who purchased a policy many years ago, I hope you never have (another) premium hike. But in the event you do, I want you to make an informed decision about what to do.

I understand the frustration. I would be angry too! But I do not want you to compound the problem by making an emotional decision that does not serve the best interests of an older you.

As I have explained here, even at an increased premium cost, your total costs would likely still be less than a year or two of long-term care. If you can afford the premium hike, I recommend swallowing hard and keeping the policy.

If the premium increase is going to be a budget buster, I encourage every one of you with adult children to discuss this with them. I respect that this may not be an easy conversation to start, but it can lead to the best outcome for your family. If you drop the policy, your kids may eventually bear the financial burden of caring for you. If their budgets allow it, I suspect they may actually be grateful to pitch in with the premium costs today. They will respect that you are actively and pragmatically planning for the future. And they may recognize that contributing toward your LTC insurance premiums now can save all of you down the line.

You can also reduce your premium costs by changing the level of coverage in your policy. You can reduce your total benefit, how many days you agree to pay out of pocket before coverage kicks in (the elimination period), or the inflation rider on your policy. Please carefully consider any changes. And ask for all possible options. For instance, if you have a 5% inflation rider, my advice is to keep it. But if the policy is just too expensive, ask if there is a 2% or 3% inflation rider option. It will be less expensive but will give you some protection from rising costs.

YOUR ULTIMATE RETIREMENT CHECKLIST

❏ Make it your goal to retire debt free.

❏ Spend less by focusing on living below your means.

❏ Make paying for your retirement a priority over borrowing for a child's college.

❏ Consider saving in tax-free retirement accounts: Roth 401(k), Roth IRA, HSA.

❏ Start working on your plan for how you will keep working until you are 70.

❏ Research long-term care insurance.

CHAPTER 4

WHERE TO LIVE

I imagine some of you are thinking you might breeze right past this chapter. You are sure you don't need any advice on where to live. You have that all figured out: You are not moving. Period.

I hear you.

I am well aware that "aging in place" has been held out as a goal, a symbol of your self-sufficiency and independence. Of course, in theory it is incredibly appealing: Staying in the house you love, and where you may have raised a family, the place of the best memories of your life, seems to be all about security and comfort. I hear so many of you saying this is exactly what you want to do. It may make terrific sense. But you need to know for sure that staying put is going to work for you long term. Financially, physically, and emotionally.

If you are intent on not moving, I insist that you make paying off your mortgage before retirement a priority. Another consideration if you intend to stay in your home is to tackle remodeling work today that will accommodate the needs of an older version of you.

However, for those of you with financial anxieties about retirement, I hope you will hear me out on the value of making a move sooner rather than later.

Reducing your housing costs now is like opening the release valve on a pressure cooker.

If you have yet to retire, reducing your housing costs in the near future will give you more cash right now to put toward other retirement goals. Maybe that's saving more for retirement. Maybe that's paying off any lingering debts. Or maybe it's the money you need to make it possible to wait until age 70 to claim Social Security.

Then, once you are retired, the fact that you have lower housing costs means you will need less income in retirement for this essential expense. Plus, you will have freed up more income for other retirement expenses. That could mean more travel. Or building up your savings so you can have all the care you need to stay in your home for as long as possible (hopefully forever!). Or spoiling the grandkids (a bit more) and donating to causes you hold dear.

Let's reframe this proposition: Considering a move that can save you money is not about what you are giving up today. It is all about what you can gain for years—the peace of mind that comes with not having to stress about money. The decision of where you live has the potential to give you the freedom to live life more exuberantly.

Ready to hear me out?

This chapter is in two sections. The first will guide you through key considerations on whether staying put is the best decision. The second section explores how making a move can pay off, and includes some outside-the-box possibilities that I hope will become more mainstream in the future.

THE MOVES TO MAKE TO DECIDE WHERE TO LIVE

If You Plan to Stay Put:

- Pay off the mortgage before you retire.

- Be able to pay your essential living costs from guaranteed income.

- Don't rely on a reverse mortgage to pay the bulk of your expenses.

- Consider whether your home will be socially isolating to an 80-plus you.

- Think through whether your home will be physically challenging for an older you (and your friends).

If You're Considering Moving:

- Do the math on the upside of financially downsizing.

- Look at the case for moving now.

- Consider making it a family (or friendly) affair.

IF YOU PLAN TO STAY PUT

Pay off the mortgage before you retire.

The only way I can endorse staying in your home is if you have the mortgage paid off before you retire. Even though I have already explained that I want you to keep working until you are 70, my recommendation is to aim to have your mortgage paid off by 65. That will give you some much-needed financial breathing room if you want to take—or are pushed into—a different job in your 60s that pays less.

Unfortunately, retiring with mortgage debt is becoming more common. About one in three homeowners between the ages of 65 and 74 still have a mortgage, and nearly 25% of people who are at least 75 have a mortgage.

That's a lot of near-retirees and retirees making a doubly bad decision, in my opinion.

The first problem is that you make your financial life a lot harder if you must continue to pay a mortgage when you are retired. Property tax, insurance, and maintenance are going to take a big enough bite out of your income. A mortgage payment on top of that will likely eat up way too much of the money you can safely spend in retirement.

In the next chapter I am going to make a strong pitch for being able to cover your basic living costs from guaranteed sources of income, such as Social Security and a pension. If you have a hefty mortgage payment, you will find it difficult to follow that advice.

If you are thinking you have plenty of money in your retirement investment accounts to tap to cover your mortgage (and other expenses), I want you to be very careful. For starters, it is likely the bulk of your retirement savings is in traditional accounts, not Roth accounts. That means that every dollar you withdraw will be taxed as income. So what does that mean in practical terms? It means that every dollar you need to withdraw to cover your mortgage payment needs to be increased to cover your tax bill. For example, if you have a $1,000 monthly mortgage payment, you might need to withdraw at least $1,200 a month to have $1,000 left after paying tax.

As I explain in Chapter 6, I think anyone retiring in the next few years should aim to spend just 3% of their portfolio in the first year of retirement and then adjust that amount for inflation in subsequent years. You may find it very hard to follow my sleep-well-at-night advice if you need more money to cover the mortgage payment.

Let's go back to my example of having a $1,000 monthly mortgage. I want you to understand that if you intend to rely on your traditional retirement accounts to cover the mortgage, and you follow my 3% spending recommendation early in retirement, you would need to have about $500,000 in those retirement accounts *just to cover your mortgage costs.* That's a lot! And just to cover the mortgage!

Are you sure you have enough in your retirement accounts to keep your spending to my 3% target when you retire and generate enough to cover your mortgage payments, let alone other living costs?

Do you now see why I think it is so much smarter to get the mortgage paid off before you retire?

I have one more sales pitch for why I want you to get the mortgage paid off before you retire: You will be happier. I have yet to meet a retiree who paid off their mortgage before they retired and regretted it. Don't minimize the emotional lift from knowing you won't have a mortgage payment to cover when you are retired.

Now, that said, you also must factor in whether you can afford to stay in the home even after paying off the mortgage. That's what we tackle next. I also am going to ask you to dig deep and think through whether staying put will be emotionally and physically kind to an older you. If staying put makes sense, please read my advice in the box on page 85 on how to find the cash today to pay off your mortgage before you retire.

MAKE SURE YOU CAN AFFORD TO STAY PUT

Even if you are on course to have your mortgage paid off, we need to make sure it really makes financial sense for you to stay in your current home.

Are you sure you can handle the annual property tax and insurance for your home? Not just today, but years from now?

And let's keep in mind that you're not the only one aging. Your home is aging too, which means more wear and tear on top of the regular maintenance costs. How old are your roof and HVAC system? If your intention is to stay in your home for 20 or more years, the reality is that you will likely have major maintenance expenses.

And please consider what tasks you do today that you might not want to—or be able to—keep doing long into retirement. Snowblowing, gardening, regular housekeeping, and general upkeep.

All of these costs can add up and back you into a corner financially.

One of the best ways to navigate through a bear market when you are retired is to give yourself the flexibility to spend less when your portfolio is down. Sure, you will still need to make the required minimum withdrawals by April 1 after the year you turn 70½ if you were born on or before 6/30/49, or 72 if you were born after, but if you are taking out more than the RMD in order to cover your housing costs, you won't have the ability to reduce your withdrawals to the RMD level in bad markets. It can also be smart when your portfolio is down to reinvest some of your RMD. If you still have to make the mortgage payment, you may not have the flexibility to do that.

Moreover, I see too many people forgetting about inflation. Even if property tax rates where you live don't rise—and that's a big if in many states in need of more revenue—what you owe will rise along with your home's assessed value. (If you live in a state [or county] that gives a property tax break to older homeowners, please make sure you understand the eligibility rules and what the net benefit may be for you.) And insurance rates rise with inflation, to say nothing of the cost of replacing a roof or paying someone to handle the snowblowing for you.

Let's assume your current carrying costs total $1,000 a month. And let's also assume that inflation rises at an annualized 3% rate. I realize that's a bit higher than what we've experienced for the past 10 years or so, but I think when it comes to "safe" retirement planning, we should be conservative in our assumptions. The long-term inflation rate over decades is around 3%.

What costs you $1,000 a month today will cost you around $1,350 in 10 years. In 20 years the monthly cost adjusted for inflation will be around $1,800. If you are 60 or younger, you need to think about your financial well-being 30 years from now. That $1,000 a month now will cost you around $2,400.

This is such an important stand-in-the-truth moment. If you are currently cutting it close when it comes to affording the carrying costs of your home, how confident are you that you will be able to afford it in the future?

As I will explain in Chapter 7, investing a portion of your portfolio in stocks is an important way to generate gains over the long term that can outpace inflation. But we all know from experience that in any given month or year, the market can dip.

Be able to pay your essential living costs from guaranteed income.

That's why I am a big believer that all your essential living costs—housing, groceries, utilities—should be paid for from guaranteed income: Social Security, a pension payout, an income annuity you purchase at retirement.

If you have the savings and steady income to cover the rising costs of owning this home, then staying put may be a great decision. But if the rising cost of staying in this home is going to make it hard for you to stay financially secure, why would you put yourself in that stressful position?

Notice I said "this home." If it is very important to you to own a home rather than renting, I appreciate that that's a priority for you. My advice, though, is to consider financially downsizing to a home that will be easy for you to afford on your retirement income. And for those of you in high-maintenance homes, I have to say that a condo or townhome can be a great choice. With a condo or townhome, you won't have the maintenance responsibilities of a single-family home, and the development may have amenities such as a gym or pool that appeal. You may also find it comforting to have neighbors nearby as you age.

Learn more about the financial questions you need to ask before you purchase a condo or townhome at my website: suzeorman.com /retirement.

Don't rely on a reverse mortgage to pay the bulk of your expenses.

Those of you who have been with me for years know I have not been a fan of reverse mortgages. In the past they were downright dangerous, as slick marketing and weak regulations caused many retirees to lose their homes.

In recent years, though, a lot has changed. The Federal Housing Administration (FHA), which insures the most popular type of reverse mortgage—called the *Home Equity Conversion Mortgage (HECM)*, has put new rules in place that protect retirees from some of the biggest problems that existed in the past.

The new rules have softened me a bit on reverse mortgages. A reverse mortgage may be a smart way to create extra income in retirement by using some of your home's equity. One big advantage of a reverse is that the income you receive is tax free. That can be a big help in retirement.

But I want to be very, very clear: A reverse mortgage only makes sense in very specific situations. There are still risks involved, which I will explain in a moment. Those may be worthwhile risks for you, but only if you go in with eyes wide-open to what you are doing.

What follows is a short course in how reverse mortgages work and how you might consider using them. If after reading this you are interested in a reverse, I don't recommend you contact a mortgage lender who specializes in reverse mortgages. Not yet. A lender is motivated to close the deal. You're not ready for that.

This is where hiring a financial planner to help you crunch the numbers, understand the risks, and consider your alternatives will be money well spent. This is such a big decision that having a reputable pro to consult with is important before you talk to a lender.

WHEN A REVERSE IS A BAD IDEA

Before we dive into the details, I want to be very clear about who should definitely not consider this. A reverse mortgage is a bad idea if:

- You need the reverse to cover the majority of your fixed living costs in your 60s and early 70s.

- You will be hard pressed to keep up with rising property tax, insurance, and maintenance costs.

- You think there's a good chance you might move in less than 5 to 10 years.

- You intend to use the money for wants (vacations, RVs) and not needs.

- You will use the money to pay off credit card debt.

- You intend to invest the money you receive.

REVERSE MORTGAGE BASICS

A reverse mortgage is a way to tap equity in your home while you still live in it. It's more reliable than a home equity line of credit (HELOC). As some of you may have experienced, HELOCs can be reduced or frozen. That's what happened to plenty of HELOC borrowers during the financial crisis of 2008.

And a HELOC can only be tapped for a set number of years—10 is typical—before you must repay the money you used.

Once you have a reverse mortgage, lenders can't change the terms. And you never have to repay any of the money you use while you remain in the house. It is only when you move, or die, that the borrowed money must be repaid. Typically, you—or your heirs—sell the house. You or your heirs will never owe more than the market value of the home when it is sold. If the sale price is more than the balance of your reverse, you or your heirs get to keep the difference.

To take out a reverse, you must first have your primary mortgage paid off. You can use proceeds from the reverse to repay any remaining mortgage balance or outstanding home equity line of credit. That only makes sense if you have a small remaining balance and will still have plenty of money left over from the reverse that you can use in retirement, when needed. That's because reverse mortgages have higher fees than a standard mortgage.

The amount you can borrow is determined by the appraised value of your home, interest rates when you take out the loan, the remaining balance on your current mortgage (and any home equity loans or lines), and your age. You must be at least 62. If you are married, just one of you needs to be 62. The amount you can borrow is a percentage of the appraised value of your home; the upper limit for a reverse mortgage backed by the FHA is $765,500. The older you are, the more you will be allowed to borrow.

Your FICO scores don't come into play with a reverse. That said, you will need to divulge all your financial information; lenders are required to make sure you will have the income to continue paying your property tax and insurance and to maintain the home. If there is any question on that front, they can require that a portion of your reverse be set aside to cover those costs. When you take out a reverse, the lender will likely charge you an "origination" fee; the FHA caps that fee at $6,000. You will also typically encounter many of the standard other "closing costs" for a loan, such as an appraisal and documentation fees.

While you will never be required to pay back money while you remain in the home, interest is charged monthly and added to your tab.

The only way to qualify for a fixed rate reverse mortgage is to choose to take the money in a lump sum. However, I don't want you to take a lump sum from a reverse mortgage. If you want to do a reverse, it should be either a line of credit or a steady monthly payout. Those types of reverse mortgages charge a variable interest rate. Again, I want to stress that you aren't required to pay back any money you use as long as you stay in the house. But with a variable rate loan, if interest rates rise, the cost of using your equity rises. That means when you or your heirs eventually sell the home, you will have less (or no) profit after paying back the reverse.

Again, you won't ever have to pay back the interest while you remain in the house. The worst-case scenario is that when you do move, or die, there will be no equity left for your heirs after the loan is paid back. (I don't think that should be a front-of-mind concern. Your job in retirement is to make sure you can live comfortably into your 90s and beyond. What you leave to your family is less important than your quality of life while you are alive.)

The chief risk with a reverse is that it is only effective while you remain in the house. Once you move out for 12 months, the lender has the right to "call" the loan and be repaid. Moving out can be from a sale or moving to assisted living or a nursing home. You can't keep the home or rent it out if you are not living there.

If you are married and your spouse is on the deed to the house and is listed as a borrower on the HECM, the reverse stays in effect for as long as one of you is in the home. This is a great change that was made a few years ago. Before then, spouses not on the HECM were forced to move when the borrower either died or moved to a care facility.

I know you have every intention of staying in your home forever, but you also know life doesn't always work according to our wishes. If you find that you need to move at some point and you have spent the money from a reverse mortgage, you may find yourself in a tough financial situation, as you will need to repay the reverse, which will leave you with less money—possibly none—to pay for where you are moving.

This becomes even more of an issue for a surviving spouse. If she (it is usually she) can't afford to keep the house, or doesn't want to stay in it, she faces the same problem with having to repay the used portion of the reverse. That could make it difficult for her to afford another place to live.

These are crucially important possibilities to consider. The Retirement Researcher website is a good resource for learning more about reverse mortgages (retirementresearcher.com/category/reverse-mortgages).

Consider whether your home will be socially isolating to an 80-plus you.

I understand that right now your home feels like a perfect fit. If you have lived there for years, it is brimming with so many memories. And for those of you whose kids have moved into their adult lives, it is often quite literally the home base that brings you all together.

I am going to ask you to tackle a tough homework assignment: Carve out some time to think about how this fantastic house will work for you when you are 80 or 85.

If you no longer can drive, or want to drive, is there convenient public transportation, taxis, Uber/Lyft so you can get around easily? How far do you live from town, or friends? Right now I bet you don't give a moment's thought to the 15- or 20-minute drive to meet up with friends, see a movie, or shop. But if we're being honest, that could become a bit much for an older you, especially if it entails driving on a busy highway. And think about those friends; they are going to age as well. Will it be easy for them to come your way?

Isolation can ruin your retirement. As sensitive as I am to the enormous challenge a move may feel like today, I have to tell you, I am way more concerned about the emotional challenges you may face if you *don't* move.

I am asking you to think this through today, not file it away as something you will deal with later, when the time comes. Believe me, years from now you will find a move even more daunting. You may have less perspective and be reluctant to acknowledge that your home is no longer a good fit. So you will stay and languish. Or your family will insist on a change, which is not a dynamic I wish on you, nor should you wish it on your children.

This is not something you can figure out in a weekend. My advice is that you begin to think about it rationally now, using your good common sense and an open mind. I also want you to open your heart to the possibility that a move might be a wonderful insurance policy that will keep you happy and safe long into retirement. If you are married, you definitely need to start talking about this as a couple. And I ask that you include in those conversations an honest assessment of what each of you envisions you may want—and need—if your spouse dies first. You may find that a move now will make that transition so much easier.

Think through whether your home will be physically challenging for an older you (and your friends).

The steps up to your front door are likely not something you even think about today. Or the fact that you must climb stairs to your bedroom. Or how you step into the tub to take a shower. An older home with a narrow entrance hall may be full of charm, but if you or your friends relied on a walker or a wheelchair, would you or they find it hard to move around?

SUZE'S STORY

I want to tell you why I am going into such detail on this topic. I am dealing with this very same issue in my family. It is not easy to accept the fact that the home we love may no longer be a safe and easy place to live. Health issues are preventing some of my family members from being able to go up and down stairs easily, so they are having to confront the reality that they may have to leave their home sooner than they'd anticipated. When KT and I built our current home, we made it all one level so stairs would not be a problem for us as we aged. This is advice I have already followed for myself!

With this is mind, now is the perfect time to think through how inviting—or not—your home will be to an older you. I recommend that you come up with a plan now that will make your home more practical.

A bedroom on the main floor (or a room that can be easily transformed into a bedroom) and a bathroom with a walk-in shower that has a bench or room for a stool are not mere niceties—they can be what allows you to stay in your home longer.

We all know that illness increases with age. Joints get creakier. Falls happen. My challenge to you is to look around your house and see how plausible and comfortable it will be to stay in your home if you become ill, arthritic, or injured.

What you want to avoid is waiting for something to happen and then being stuck in a home that is not ready to take care of you. After a fall that breaks a hip, you don't have months to wait to get a permit—and contractors—to put in a ramp where there are now stairs into your home. If you must step into a bathtub, how's that going to work if you become very arthritic? You want a shower you can access without such a big step up and down. Ideally you should have a bathroom that has the space for a walker or wheelchair.

There are also changes you can make today that can help prevent accidents inside your home: better lighting, more light switches so you're never walking a step in the dark, replacing throw rugs with wall-to-wall carpet (tripping is a huge problem), and professionally installed grab bars in the bathroom.

And then there are the quality of life changes. Lever door handles are a lot easier to manage than regular knobs if you have arthritis. Laundry in the basement? That likely isn't much fun today; imagine what it will feel like in 15 or 20 years. Installing a lower countertop in the kitchen can make it easy to lower countertop in the kitchen can make it easy to do food prep without having to stand; it also has the added benefit of being ideal for young grandchildren to hang out and cook with you.

Those are just a few age-in-place projects to consider. The National Association of Home Builders (NAHB) has a checklist. (Plug "NAHB aging in place remodeling checklist" into your web browser.")

Even if you are a decade or two from retiring, I think it's smart to start thinking about changes you will want to have in place for an older you. If you are in your 50s and tackling a renovation project, why not add designs and fixtures that will work for an older you?

If you want to scope out possible projects, be sure to ask contractors if they have experience or training in renovation projects to keep a home safe for aging owners. This is becoming a very big part of the home-renovation industry; the NAHB offers a Certified Aging-in-Place Specialist (CAPS) designation. To find a CAPS professional in your area, visit nahb.org /designationsdirectory and then select "CAPS."

If you are in your 50s or 60s and still working, paying for a major project will likely make more sense today. Ideally you would finance everything from your current cash flow and nonemergency savings. But if you need to borrow, it is going to be easier to qualify for a personal loan or home equity line of credit (HELOC) while you are working, and then get it paid off before you retire.

Once you are 59½, you can make withdrawals from traditional retirement plans without paying an early withdrawal penalty, though you will owe income tax. Also remember that money you originally put into a Roth IRA can be withdrawn tax free at any time regardless of your age or how long that account has been open.

However, withdrawing money from retirement savings for renovations must be carefully considered. Money you pull out earlier is money you no longer have growing for you to generate income in your retirement.

That said, judiciously spending some money that enables you to stay in your home for a few more years—and hopefully forever—can be a wise investment. As I shared in Chapter 3, the current average cost of an assisted living facility is about $50,000 a year, and a private room in a nursing home costs an average of $100,000 a year. Spending $25,000 or $50,000 or even more on "age-in-place" renovations that might keep you in this home longer can pay off financially, not to mention emotionally.

But before you agree to a costly project, you must, must, must run the numbers to calculate whether you will still have sufficient savings left in your retirement accounts to generate the income you will need when you are retired (Chapter 6). It is crucial to consider the opportunity cost of spending money today that will reduce your retirement accounts. Again, a reputable financial planner can be an excellent resource to help you weigh your options.

This is yet another pivotal stand-in-your-truth moment. I understand how much you want to stay in your home, but if the cost to make it safe and comfortable for an older you means dangerously eating into your retirement savings, I want you to reconsider. Moving may just be the best thing you can do to ensure that you have the money you need for your 80s and 90s.

HOW TO PAY OFF YOUR MORTGAGE BEFORE AGE 65

If you are confident you can—and want to—remain in your home, you must move forward with a plan to be debt free no later than 65.

The first step is to contact your current loan servicer and ask for a new "amortization schedule" that will have your loan paid off by the time you are 65.

That's simply what your monthly payments need to be to get the balance to zero by no later than age 65. When you start making the new payments, be sure the loan servicer is applying 100% of the extra amount to your principal, and none of the extra payment to interest. Not sure where to come up with the extra cash to make those higher payments?

On the next two pages are my recommendations. The order is intentional. Always opt for 1 before considering 2. And 2 before 3.

---

1. Find more monthly cash flow to put toward your mortgage payment.

Don't tell me you have no give in your spending. Everyone does. It's a matter of priorities. And your priority now is to get the mortgage paid off. In Chapter 2 we discussed how recalibrating your spending on family could free up much-needed dollars, and in Chapter 3 I laid out strategies big and small for how you can reduce your spending.

2. Use excess cash savings.

I have long advised that an emergency fund should be large enough to cover your basic living expenses for eight months. That is especially true for everyone over the age of 50: If you find yourself pushed out of a job, it can often take longer to find another job, and it will often be at a lower salary.

But if you have more than eight months' savings—and I am always pleasantly surprised by how many 50-plus households do—I recommend you consider using some of the excess to pay down your mortgage balance.

It makes less sense to have extra money earning a low interest rate when it could be used to pay off a debt that is charging you a higher interest rate. Let's say you are super smart and have your savings at an online savings bank or at a credit union; these days they are paying close to 2% interest. That interest is taxable income, so let's assume the net after-tax yield is in the vicinity of 1.6%.

You can't tell me your mortgage rate is less than that. Even if you refinanced when rates were rock bottom in the wake of the financial crisis, you're still paying around 3.5%. If you are getting a full tax write-off for the mortgage interest, even if you are in the 32% tax bracket, after taxes you are still paying 2.4%, which is more than that money you are saving is earning.

And the reality is that after the 2017 tax reform bill, most of you are no longer itemizing anyway. Many of you are now better off filing a federal tax return that claims the standard deduction ($12,400 for individuals, $24,800 for married couples filing a joint return for the 2020 tax year) rather than itemizing your deductions. If you've stopped claiming the mortgage interest deduction, then holding on to this mortgage makes even less sense.

And for those of you who still itemize, the math doesn't likely support holding on to the mortgage. For starters, if your 30-year fixed rate mortgage is at least 15 years old, you are now paying more principal than interest. So the dollar value of the interest you could deduct is falling each year. Again, even if you are at a high federal tax bracket of, say, 32%, the dollar value of the deduction is going to be less than the savings you could pocket if you were no longer paying interest on a mortgage.

3. Use Roth IRA savings.

If over the years you have saved money in a Roth IRA, you can make tax-free withdrawals of both your contributions and your earnings once you are 59½ and the Roth account is at least five years old. (Prior to 59½, you can withdraw any money you originally contributed without taxes or penalties regardless of how long the account has been open. The only potential tax is on earnings; if you withdraw earnings before the account is five years old or before you reach age 59½, you will owe tax.) Using tax-free money to pay off your mortgage makes more sense than pulling money out of traditional 401(k)s and IRAs that will not only be taxed as income but could bump you into a higher tax bracket.

4. Reduce what you're contributing to workplace retirement accounts.

For those of you who are still working and contributing to a workplace retirement account, I want you to scale back those contributions after the point when your company stops matching so you have more money to put toward accelerating your mortgage payoff. Surprised? Let's talk this through together. You may be thinking you need to build your retirement accounts as large as possible to have a shot at the income you need in retirement. But let's consider those income needs: If you get rid of the mortgage cost, the monthly income you need to cover your living expenses just dropped dramatically.

It's also crucial to realize that every dollar you withdraw from traditional 401(k)s and IRAs will be taxed as income. If you have a $1,000 monthly mortgage, as we noted above, you might need to withdraw $1,200 or so to net the $1,000 after tax.

At this stage of your life, if staying in your home is a priority, I recommend contributing only enough to your workplace plan to qualify for the company matching contribution. That is a deal you never want to pass up.

Once you reduce your contribution to the match level, your after-tax take-home pay will rise. I want you to use every dollar of that increase to go toward your mortgage payment. Even though you are paying tax on more income, this move can still make sense if it gives you the peace of mind of having your mortgage paid off before you retire. Believe me: I think many of you will be so happy to not have to worry about a mortgage in retirement.

IF YOU'RE CONSIDERING MOVING

Do the math on the upside of financially downsizing.

As I mentioned at the beginning of this chapter, reducing your housing expenses has a double payoff. It will help with your immediate cash flow, giving you more money each month to use for other priorities. And it effectively reduces your retirement housing costs, which will leave more of your retirement income for other expenses. Or it can be the difference between being able to afford to retire comfortably, and not.

If you intend to work for 10 more years, there are so many great moves a financial downsize might unleash.

Let's say you reduce your housing costs by 25%. For example, if you spend $2,000 a month today, here's what you might be able to use that $500 in savings for:

- If you have any lingering debts, you've just given yourself the means to dig out.

- Been meaning to build up your emergency fund? Adding $6,000 a year for a few years is going to feel pretty amazing.

- Did my pitch for long-term care insurance in Chapter 3 resonate, but you're worried about the cost? A financial downsize today can free up more than enough money to pay the premium today and also save some money to help continue paying the premium throughout your retirement.

- As I have already noted, delaying Social Security payments until you are 70 is one of the best retirement planning moves you can make, yet it may seem impractical if you can't imagine continuing to work that long in a demanding job. When you lower your housing costs, you may unleash the flexibility to choose a different job, one that you actually look forward to, even if it pays less. That not only helps you patiently wait to claim Social Security; I think for many, it will lift your spirits to move you past your current grind.

- Have children and grandchildren living a flight away? You just increased your family travel budget. Or perhaps you use the money to save up for a few bucket-list trips that are now financially feasible.

- Wish you had some tax-free savings for retirement? If you qualify for a Roth IRA, saving $500 a month for 10 years and earning an annualized 5% would give you more than $75,000 in tax-free money for retirement. In 2020, individuals at least 50 years old with modified adjusted gross income below $124,000 and married couples with income below $196,000 could save $7,000 in a Roth IRA. If you make too much to qualify for a Roth IRA but have a workplace retirement plan, check whether there is a Roth option. Many 401(k) plans now have a Roth option, where you contribute after-tax dollars and then will have tax-free income in retirement. There are no income limits to contribute to a Roth 401(k).

Those are just some of my notions. I hope you are excited by what might be possible if you financially downsize sooner rather than later.

Now I say that knowing that for some of you, the emotional ties to this house—your house—seem too strong to sever. You and I are experienced enough in life to know that trade-offs are how we navigate our worlds. Will you miss your home? Maybe? Okay, probably, at least initially. Change isn't necessarily easy. But you aren't just giving up this home. You are giving yourself a new home that may be an even better fit for you now, and if it also helps you financially, how can that not be an exciting proposition?

Are you mostly staying put because of Thanksgiving and Christmas? You know what I am talking about: This home is where your family still comes together for holidays. This home is where traditions are honored and memories are created. I understand how that can make a move seem excruciatingly hard to consider.

But I am asking you to open your head and heart a bit. Memories travel with you, and many of the traditions will too. For it is the people, not the place, that bind us close to those we love.

A move does not wipe out those traditions and memories. And your family will still gather. Maybe at your new home. Maybe the adult kids have been itching to step into the holiday host role. New traditions and memories are waiting to happen wherever you are.

Worried your family will be sad if you "give up" this house? I get it; the more special the life you created in this house, the harder it is for everyone to let go. But I ask you—and them—to consider the next chapter. Knowing you are in a new home that is going to work for you financially and physically is an amazing gift a parent can give an adult child. You do know they worry about you, right?

As you explain your motivations for making a change, I think your kids will be so happy that you are proactively seeking out change that will give you more security, more safety down the line, and best of all, the chance to worry less.

There are a number of ways to financially downsize. If you want to buy another home, your goal should be to be able to afford a new home without a mortgage.

When you sell a home that was your principal residence for at least two of the last five years, the first $250,000 in profit is tax free ($500,000 for married couples). Above that level you will owe long-term capital gains tax, which will likely be either 0% or 15% based on current rates. (To calculate your gain, you add all the cost of improvements you put into the house over the years to the original sale price. For example, if you paid $100,000 and have the records to show $50,000 in renovation projects—a new HVAC, a new roof, etc.—you will report $150,000 as the adjusted cost of your home and then figure out your gain from there.)

To make that possible, you might move to a smaller place in the same town, or a few towns over. Or perhaps you are considering an interstate retirement move. I am all for a move to a less expensive region, but please don't let finances be your only consideration. You need to want to be there. Saving money yet being miserable is a horrible trade-off.

As I explain later, I also think there is a tremendous opportunity to save a lot of money and build in a tight social and logistical support system by considering moving in with family or friends. Hold on! I know that won't work for everyone. But I want those of you who reflexively know that might work for you to understand that I am 100% with you on this.

Renting may be a way to financially downsize; it can also make sense if you are considering a move to a new life—suburb to city, or city to suburb—that you want to test out for a few years.

It can also be a temporary step if you are still working and plan to move elsewhere later. If you sell now and rent, you have tucked away the money for your future home. Or you could use the money to buy the home where you intend to retire and rent it out to earn some income until you are ready to move in yourself.

More seniors are renting these days, catching on to not just the economics but the ease that comes with no longer having to be in charge of maintenance.

Now all that said, renting has its obvious trade-offs—mainly, rising rents—but if you are a home-owner, your property tax, utilities, maintenance, and insurance will cost more over the years as well.

Choosing to rent can also give a needed late-stage boost to your retirement savings. You likely have a ballpark figure in mind of what you could walk away with after selling your home.

That could be a whole lot of extra retirement security. In Chapter 7 I explain how to invest during retirement. That advice is what you should follow if you sell your home and have profit you can invest.

IS A CONTINUING CARE RETIREMENT COMMUNITY A GOOD FIT FOR YOU?

Retirement communities have been evolving to address the changing housing and care needs that increased longevity brings. A Continuing Care Retirement Community (CCRC) offers residents access to increasing levels of assistance. You move to a CCRC as a fully independent resident, often to a condo-like apartment. Meals are in a dining room, and there are lots of activities, which you can partake in or ignore. You're in charge. Many CCRCs are packed with amenities, including gyms, pools, and movie theaters.

On the campus of your CCRC, there will also be assisted living facilities; some offer memory care and nursing-home care. If your needs change as you age, you will be able to move to a different part of the same CCRC campus.

SUZE'S STORY

When my mom was about 87, she was still living alone in Chicago. She and her friend Esther had hatched a plan that they would move to a CCRC in Florida that Esther had heard about. My mom told me about it and was so excited to go.

Then Esther died before they made the move. Before she died, Esther made my mom promise to proceed with the plan to move to Florida.

My mom asked KT and me to look into it. We were still living in San Francisco at the time, so we flew to Florida with the intention of taking a look at the place to see if there was an apartment that would be a great fit for my mom.

Then we took it one step further. We rented the unit and moved in for one full week. We ate in the restaurant where everyone ate. We swam in the pool (actually, it was the only time I didn't care about being seen in a bathing suit), we went to the movies and the games rooms, we sat in on interesting lectures, and we made a point to talk to residents. We loved it. And so did my mom for the 10 years she lived there.

It was a great decision for her, and it's how KT and I ended up moving to Florida, since my mom wanted us nearby. Whenever I would ask her if she missed her life in Chicago, she said, "Are you kidding me? Who would miss Chicago winters?"

There are a variety of ways you can pay to live at a CCRC. Some allow you to rent—like my mom did—and then pay more as time goes on if you need more care. Others charge an up-front entry fee that essentially "buys" you more care as the years go on. If you go that route, it's likely you will need to use the profit from selling your existing home to cover the fee. You also have options on what level of care you want to purchase: soup-to-nuts coverage or pay-as-you-go. One pricing model gives you a limited number of days of stepped-up care. You can also purchase a basic level of care if you already have a long-term care insurance policy that you will tap if the need arises to have support.

The myLifesite website (www.mylifesite.net /resources) provides research on more than 800 CCRCs and offers advice on how to vet CCRCs and find the right financial fit. It is run by Brad Breeding, a certified financial planner who is paid by myLifesite customers, not the CCRCs. There is free educational material on the site, and you can get basic information about CCRCs there. For more detailed analysis and access to the site's calculators, the cost is $29 a month. Breeding also wrote a book that walks through the basics of CCRCs: *What's the Deal with Retirement Communities?*

Look at the Case for Moving Now

As I write this in late 2019, most regions of the country are experiencing strong housing markets. That makes now a very good time to consider downsizing.

Could prices rise even more in the next three to five years? Of course. Could they fall? Maybe. Could the market in your area weaken if we find ourselves in an economic recession? Absolutely.

I have no crystal ball that tells me what is going to happen. No one does. My concern is that you not fall into the trap of focusing only on the potential upside of waiting to make a move.

You can do yourself so many favors if you simply ask yourself this question: *What happens if I am wrong?*

If you are thinking about staying in your home for a few more years because you anticipate being able to sell it for more if you wait, then you should stand in the truth of considering the possibility that things don't pan out as expected.

If a move makes sense today and the only reason you are holding on is to maybe "get more" later, you are taking a risk.

And to be clear, let's say you do sell this year or next, and five years from now values are even higher. Will that mean you have made a mistake? I don't think so. If you are moving to solidify your retirement finances, to free up more cash for other important goals, or to settle into a home that is going to be comfortable and safe for an older you, you would be nuts to characterize that as a mistake.

If you expect your gain to be more than $250,000 ($500,000 for married couples who file a joint return), I also think it's worth considering the chance that the long-term capital gains rate could rise in the future. Again, none of us has a crystal ball, especially when it comes to anticipating what Washington might do. But keep in mind that the current tax law expires after 2025. I wouldn't be surprised if today's low tax rates are increased in the coming years, given the size of our national debt.

Right now the long-term capital gains tax rate is low. It is based on your income in the year you have the gain. As you can see in the table below, that is likely going to be no more than 15%.

LONG-TERM CAPITAL GAINS TAX RATES		
Capital Gains Rate	Single Filer Income	Married Filing Jointly Income
0%	$0 – $39,999	$0 – $79,999
15%	$40,000 – $441,450	$80,000 – $496,600
20%	$441,451+	$496,601+

If you have very high income, I recommend checking with your tax pro to understand your total tax bill. In some instances the excess gain from a home sale may be subject to the net investment income tax.

Consider making it a family (or friendly) affair.

If you have money anxiety and are open to making a move, I encourage you to think a bit out of the box. Especially those of you who are single.

What if you lived with an adult child? A sibling? A friend (or two, or three)?

Please don't immediately dismiss this without giving it some serious consideration. I think there is so much upside to living with family or friends. Sharing costs is just one part of it. Socially it can be such a positive move. I appreciate that right now your life is full. But we also know that as we age, social isolation—and its fierce cousin, depression—can become serious problems.

Can't imagine your adult kids being up for this? Are you sure? Because I talk to a lot of them and they are Stressed with a capital *S*. Stressed about money. Stressed about having to work so hard and having to pay for childcare and not having enough time with their kids. Stressed about how they will juggle all of that and be able to be more present for you as you age. Sharing expenses helps with that. Being close by alleviates their stress, and—admit it—yours too.

This is an act of profound generosity that puts each of you in the position of being one who both gives and receives.

Will this work for all families? Of course not. But I am asking those of you who find this at all plausible to consider it.

Start talking. This is not a decision that is made over a weekend visit. Give yourself time to ease into the idea and consider all the options.

Your family could move in with you. Or vice versa. Or you may decide everyone will move to a new home that has the right layout. In some parts of the country, builders of new homes are working with floor plans that create private space for all adults and shared space as well.

Worried about your privacy? Perhaps building a small "in-law" unit can be a great solution, if you or the kids have the room and the zoning in your area allows for it. Maybe it's an extension to the current house, converting the garage, or an "accessory dwelling unit" (ADU), the official name for a small stand-alone structure that is catching on in many areas. If you love your house but it is too big, might it be just the right size for one of your kids and their family? If you build an ADU in the backyard, you have your privacy, they have theirs, and you are still connected to this home you love.

Any sort of construction will cost money, but it could be a terrific investment if it keeps you "home" for longer, and shared expenses will help everyone. Depending on your desire, maybe you step in and provide some care for young kids. That can be a huge financial relief for your kids, and it is a logistical godsend if they don't have to rush home or to day care at a rigid deadline each day.

Needless to say, there are many details to work out. Don't wing any of this. Everything needs to be spelled out in terms of monthly contributions of money and time (if you are helping with the kids). Who is cooking dinner? Shopping?

I also encourage you to work with a lawyer to make sure everyone is protected. We can all assume you will die first, but we know that is not always the case. Making sure your children have life insurance is important in order to provide the income needed for everyone—including you—to remain in the home.

You also want to work through ownership of the house and how it will "pass" to each other when there is a death. As I will explain in Chapter 9, owning the home within a living revocable trust is the smart way to do this. But I encourage working with a lawyer to make sure you have all the multigenerational issues regarding the home set up to make for a smooth transition.

If you don't have kids, or don't think living together is going to work, how about friends? Or other family? I think this could be such a terrific option for women.

According to Pew Research Center, more than half of women between the ages of 65 and 84 have never been married or are divorced or widowed. For men it's less than 30%.

It doesn't need to be your best friend. Compatibility is the goal. Don't have anyone in your circle you think would be open to this? You might want to check out Silvernest.com, a roommate-matching service that specializes in the 50-plus crowd (www.silvernest.com).

Having a roommate comes with all sorts of possibilities. They move into your home. You move into theirs. You both move into a new home that has the right layout for roommates and is age-in-place friendly.

There is no one template for how to do this. But the key is to err on the side of putting everything in writing. The more potential kinks you can anticipate, the better this will be for everyone.

Be specific. Everyone should make a list of their top five must-haves and the five things they can't deal with. You are going to have much in common; just take the time to work through the differences. Do you have different notions of what "clean" is? Perhaps budgeting for a housekeeper is something to consider. If there is an extra bedroom or two, what will be the house policy on visitors? Will you be cooking and food shopping together? And what are your expectations if one of you becomes very ill? Of course you will be there for each other through a surgery or illness. But you need to have a clear understanding of where the care will come from if one of you develops dementia or Alzheimer's, or another debilitating illness.

I want to circle back to where we started this chapter: The decision of where you will live can transform your retirement outlook from worried or slightly nervous to confident and happy. My hope is that you will move this decision front and center. Waiting to see what will happen is not kind to you. Delay will just make decisions harder. Talk to your family. Talk to your friends. Talk to a certified financial planner who can help you sort through all the financial moving pieces.

Then make an informed decision on what is the best place for you to live in retirement and when to make that move. Get this decision right, and I think you will be amazed by how it enriches your life, today and years from now.

YOUR ULTIMATE RETIREMENT CHECKLIST

❑ Assess whether your current home is a good financial, physical, and emotional fit for an older you.

❑ Make sure you will be able to afford the rising cost of property tax, maintenance, and insurance if you stay in your current home.

❑ Inspect your house: Will it be safe and practical for an older you?

❑ If you need to renovate for an older you, do it sooner rather than later.

❑ Pay off the mortgage before you retire, if you intend to stay put.

❑ Consider how moving could bolster your financial security.

❑ Explore new living arrangements: living with children or friends, or in a CCRC.

❑ If it is practical and you plan to move, take advantage of the current strong housing market.

CHAPTER 5

POWER MOVES FOR YOUR 60'S

When the numbers of life start to spool out from 59 to 60 to 65, and suddenly you are about to leave your 60s behind, I have to tell you, there's this feeling of disbelief, like, *How can this be? Where did all the time go?* I swear it was just yesterday that I was celebrating my 50th, and yet the calendar insists I am 68. I don't feel 68—I still feel young! It certainly is a different 68 than it was in my parents' generation.

Regardless of how you feel inside, your 60s is a decade full of transitions. Medicare kicks in at 65. Perhaps you are downshifting to a different or part-time job. Or making a move. I have plenty of advice in this chapter to help you navigate the various transitions, but I want to be clear that there is no one perfect template.

This is especially true in regard to the process for actually retiring.

For some, it will be a full-stop event similar to what your parents and grandparents likely experienced. Friday is your last day at the job and the following Monday is your first day of retirement, with absolutely no work on your agenda.

But for many there will be a more gradual transition into retirement. Sometime in your 60s, you might find yourself ready to leave the full-time job that defined your career. Or . . . you may get a push out the door.

In either case, you're not ready to stop work completely.

Psychologically you like work. You like the challenge, the routine, and the social connectedness with colleagues. But perhaps you are ready for a less demanding work routine. Maybe you'd be interested in working part time. Maybe it is consulting in your field or working freelance. Maybe it is an entirely new field that feeds your passion or gives you the opportunity to make some money from a lifelong hobby.

For many of you, there will be an economic need to keep working in some capacity. As we have already discussed, continuing to earn money through your 60s is the best way to solidify your retirement finances. If you want to work even longer, that's great. All I ask is that if you are worried about your security in retirement, that's a sign that you should make it a goal to keep earning some income until you are at least 70.

Working longer can mean you won't need to touch your retirement savings in your 60s. Or it will make it possible to make smaller withdrawals in your 60s. A hands-off approach to your investments through your 60s is a powerful way to extend the life of your portfolio so it can support you into your 90s. Working longer can also make it possible for you to wait until you are 70 to claim your Social Security retirement benefit. As we will explore in this chapter, that may turn out to be the single smartest retirement decision you can make.

If you're feeling a bit cheated or deflated by the prospect of working until you are at least 70, I think you are missing the bigger picture. Someone who retires at 70 will still likely have many years of full-blown retirement. In fact, you will probably spend many more years retired than past generations that stopped working at 65 or younger. That's why I say that when it comes to timing your retirement, 70 is the new 65.

TAKING THE LONGEVITY VIEW

The single most important factor in your retirement strategy is how long you expect to live.

If you knew for certain that you would die at 75, you would make different choices about your investing strategy and spending than if you anticipated needing money to support you until you are 95 or 100.

If you are in good health today, I want you to assume you will live to 95 and base your retirement strategy on that prospect. To be even safer, let's plan on you living to age 100.

Can't imagine living that long? I think you may be surprised at how high the odds are that you will live into your 10th decade.

- A 65-year-old woman in average health has a 44% probability of still being alive at age 90.

- A 65-year-old man in average health has a 33% probability of still being alive at age 90.

- A married couple, both age 65 and in average health, have a 62% probability that one spouse will be alive at age 90.

Those aren't small odds, right? And that's just for "average" health. If you arrive in your mid-60s in very good health, your odds of living into your 90s are even higher. And I want to be sure you carefully read what I just wrote: Those are not the odds that you will die at 90. *Those are the odds that you will still be alive.*

Of course, if you have a condition that you know for sure will reduce your life span, that is an important factor in your personal planning. But for most of you, it is a more reasonable assumption that you will be alive for a very long time. To repeat my advice: Plan on living to *at least* 95. And for those of you who relate to my personal preference for being extra safe, I think basing your retirement plan on age 100 is smart, especially if there is a history of longevity in your family.

If you need some more convincing, I recommend using the free online Longevity Illustrator (www.longevityillustrator.org). (Click the Get Started button in the upper right-hand corner.) This tool was developed by the Society of Actuaries, an organization of wonky people that pensions and insurance companies rely on to understand life span probabilities.

While you will craft a plan that's unique to you about what your 60s work life looks like, there are some universal decisions and financial moves that are crucial for everyone to make in this decade.

THE MOVES TO MAKE IN YOUR 60'S

- Decide whether a 401(k) rollover makes sense.

- Keep investing for a long retirement.

- Delay starting Social Security until age 70.

- Choose the safe pension payout option.

- Enroll in Medicare and supplemental coverage.

- Be flexible if a bear market hits early in retirement.

Decide whether a 401(k) rollover makes sense.

(*Please note*: the advice for a 401(k) applies to all defined-contribution plans such as 403(b)s and the Thrift Saving Plan for federal employees.)

If you changed jobs a few times over the course of your career, you may have more than one 401(k). When you change employers, there is no requirement that you must do anything with your 401(k)s. You can leave them where they are. But it can become a logistical hassle in retirement to manage withdrawals—and tax reporting—from multiple accounts.

The decision whether to keep your 401(k)s where they are or to consolidate them at one brokerage firm depends on your personal situation, goals, and comfort level. For some of you, consolidating is going to be a great move that streamlines administration. For others, you may find that you want to leave your 401(k)s in place. I want you to understand that this is not an all-or-nothing decision. Let's say you have three 401(k) accounts from three old jobs. You could move two of them into a rollover account and leave the third one right where it is.

To help you decide on what is right for you, let's review the pros and cons of a 401(k) rollover.

THE ADVANTAGES OF A 401(K) ROLLOVER

One Clear View

When you have retirement money sitting in different 401(k)s from a string of old jobs, it can be tough to follow a unified strategy for how much you want invested in stocks and how much in bonds. If you move all those accounts under one roof, it becomes much easier to track your asset allocation.

Potentially Lower Costs

In Chapter 7 I walk through how to invest in retirement. A key element I cover in depth is to focus on keeping your investment costs as low as possible. When you move your money into a 401(k) rollover at a low-cost brokerage, you will be able to invest in index mutual funds and exchange-traded funds (ETFs) that have very low fees. In fact, Fidelity now has a series of mutual funds that do not charge *any* annual fees.

For those of you who worked for smaller companies over the years, my bet is that the fees you are paying to own the funds in your old 401(k) could be higher than what you would pay if you did a rollover and invested in low- or no-cost index mutual funds or ETFs. The savings can add up to thousands of dollars over time.

An Easier Time Managing Withdrawals

Having all the accounts in one place can also make it easier to keep track of your withdrawals. Keep in mind that in most cases once you are 70½ (if born on or before 6/30/49) or 72 (if born after that date), you have to start making Required Minimum Distributions (RMDs) from traditional 401(k)s and IRAs by the following April 1. That was the deal you made with Uncle Sam: You got tax breaks when you contributed to those accounts, and now that you are older, the government wants to finally collect some tax on that money. (More on RMDs in Chapter 6.)

REASONS TO KEEP
YOUR MONEY IN A 401(K)

- **It has great low-cost investment options.** If you have worked for a large employer, chances are you have a lineup of low-cost funds to invest in. As I explain in Chapter 7, there are index mutual funds and ETFs that charge an annual fee—called the *expense ratio*—of 0.10% or less. If the funds in your 401(k) charge fees that low, you have one less reason to do a rollover.

- **You feel safe and secure.** Over the years that you have worked for your employer, you probably have become comfortable with the investment choices you were making. Maybe your money is already invested in a way you like and understand. You know how to read the statements and whom to talk to, and that makes you feel secure. Perhaps you are afraid that if you do a rollover, you will be on your own with a large sum of money to invest from scratch. Even though you are overseeing that large sum of money in your 401(k), there may be a comfort level in sticking with what you know. If that is important to you, then you may want to keep your money in your 401(k).

- **Protection.** There is a valuable protection embedded in your 401(k). Federal law requires that a 401(k) plan be run with your best interests as the priority. In financial speak, all 401(k)s are held to a *fiduciary standard.* This is so important. But once you move your money into a rollover, you are on your own. And if you hire someone to help you manage your investments in retirement, you need to understand that they won't necessarily have your best interests in mind. Some will, but many won't.

In Chapter 8 I tell you how to find a great financial advisor. But right now, I want you to understand that there are bad actors out there who want to steer you into investments that will pay them fat commissions and fees. That is definitely not in your best interest.

The most glaring example of a bad deal is anyone who suggests you should do a 401(k) rollover and then buy expensive insurance products that are marketed as great investments for retirement. In most cases they are only great for the person selling them, who will earn a big commission from the sale.

There are also financial advisors who earn money when they steer you into mutual funds that charge high annual expenses—they get a cut of that fee.

That's not in your best interest. It's a conflict of interest that can cost you tens of thousands of dollars over a 20- to 30-year retirement.

A few years ago, a federal agency issued a report estimating that this "conflicted" advice costs retirees $17 billion a year in higher fees.

As I explain in Chapter 8, enlisting the guidance of a good advisor to help you pull together all the puzzle pieces of your retirement can be a very wise decision. But only if you hire a pro who does not make money from any investment you buy or sell, and who recommends a portfolio that uses low-cost index funds and ETFs.

If you find yourself near retirement and being pitched by someone suggesting anything else, slow down. It is far better to do nothing than to do something you do not understand. If that means leaving your money in a 401(k) until you are clear on what you want to do, then doing nothing is the smart move.

The bottom line is that there can be great upside to a rollover, but don't be in a rush.

ROLLOVER MECHANICS

If you decide you want to move your accounts under one roof, you will first need to have a rollover account at a brokerage. Low-cost discount brokerages such as Fidelity, Schwab, TD Ameritrade, and Vanguard are good choices if you want to move retirement accounts under one roof. If you already have any accounts at one of these brokerages—or a brokerage you like—it is very easy to open a 401(k) rollover account there.

No account at a discount brokerage? Relax. The discount brokerages are eager to help you. They want your money to come under their roof! The online process is not hard to follow, but if you have questions or concerns, the customer service red carpet will be rolled out.

The correct way to move your 401(k) money from your old employer into a rollover account is through a "custodian to custodian transfer." A bit of a mouthful, but what this means is that your employer and the brokerage where you have your rollover account will work directly with each other. The brokerage will contact your employer and arrange for your 401(k) money to be moved directly into your rollover account. You are to never take physical possession of that money; that is a mistake that can create a huge tax bill.

Keep investing for a long retirement.

There is a tendency to think that when you retire, you can't afford to take any more investing risks.

You definitely want to be more conservative than you were at 35 or 45, but in the vast majority of cases, it still makes great sense to keep some of your retirement funds invested in the stock market.

In Chapter 7 I explain why stocks are important—spoiler alert: inflation!—and share some strategies for deciding how much to keep invested in stocks. Right now I just want to plant the seed that the year you retire is a big deal for you, but shouldn't be a big deal for your investment strategy. You are retiring, but your portfolio isn't. It still needs to work for you for another 25 years or more.

Delay starting Social Security until age 70.

If you are in your 60s and have yet to claim Social Security, I am thrilled! As I touched on in Chapter 3, delaying when you start to collect your Social Security benefit until the highest earner in your household is 70 is very smart, yet most households don't wait.

And you are now at an age where this decision becomes even harder, because once you are 62 you know you are able to start collecting your Social Security retirement benefit. I appreciate that it can be hard to wait, but please hear me out on why waiting is the best financial move for most of you.

While you can indeed start collecting your Social Security retirement benefit at age 62, the benefit you are entitled to at age 62 will be a lot less than if you wait until age 70. As I mentioned in Chapter 3, it is estimated that claiming Social Security at the wrong age reduces the average lifetime benefit for U.S. households by $111,000. It can be even more for higher-income households.

Did that sink in? You get six figures just for being patient!

That is why I want you to hear me loud and clear: The payoff from waiting until age 70 to start your Social Security benefit is the best investment you can make for your retirement. If you are married, the goal should be for the spouse who was the highest earner—and thus will have a higher benefit—to wait until age 70; it is less important for the other spouse to wait until age 70.

THE THREE KEY SOCIAL SECURITY AGES

Wringing the most value out of Social Security requires understanding the relationship between three pivotal ages that determine your benefit.

- **Your Full Retirement Age (FRA).** This is the age at which you are eligible to collect 100% of your earned benefit. Everyone born in 1960 and later has a FRA of 67. If you were born between 1955 and 1960, your FRA is between 66 and 67. If you were born between 1943 and 1954, your FRA is 66. (You can find your FRA at the Social Security website: www.ssa.gov/planners /retire/agereduction.html.)

- **Age 62.** This is the youngest age you are allowed to collect Social Security retirement benefits. When you claim at age 62, your benefit will be 25% to 30% *less* than what you would receive if you waited until your FRA.

- **Age 70.** This is the age when you will be eligible for the highest possible Social Security benefit. If you start collecting at age 70, your benefit will be 24% to 32% *more* than your FRA benefit.

On the Social Security website, you can use the Retirement Estimator tool to see what your benefits may be at certain ages, based on your earnings record on file (www.ssa.gov/benefits/retirement/estimator.html).

THE HIGH COST OF CLAIMING EARLY

A benefit you start at age 70 will be 76% higher than the benefit you will get if you start at age 62. That works out to an average annual benefit boost of more than 7% over the eight years. There is no investment in the world that *guarantees* you anything close to a 7% annual return. Sure, you can invest in stocks, but there is no guarantee that in eight years you will earn an annualized return of more than 7%. You might even lose money. A five-year bank certificate of deposit guarantees a return, but as I write this in late 2019, even the best deals pay less than 3% interest, as do safe Treasury bonds.

In my opinion, you are nuts to pass up the guaranteed returns that the Social Security system will pay you if you are patient.

One important caveat: If you have a medical condition that you know will shorten your life, then claiming earlier may make sense. But as I explain below, if you are married, delaying will ensure the highest possible benefit for the surviving spouse.

COLLECTING SOCIAL SECURITY WHILE YOU ARE STILL WORKING IN YOUR 60'S

I want to be clear: I consider this a serious mistake, because you are not giving yourself the chance to earn the highest possible benefit by waiting until age 70.

But if you insist on not listening to me, and you take your benefit before your FRA while you are still working, I want you to understand that you may temporarily lose some of your benefit.

If you take Social Security between the ages of 62 and your FRA, in 2020, you can earn up to $18,240 without any deduction from your benefit. Above that level your benefit will be reduced by $1 for every $2 you earn over $18,240. In the year you reach your FRA, you can earn more without this reduction; in 2020 someone who is reaching their FRA can earn $48,600 before the earnings test kicks in.

Once you reach your FRA there is no more earnings test. You can earn whatever you want without any reduction in your benefit.

If you do have your benefits reduced, the good news is that when you reach your FRA, your benefit will be recalculated to essentially pay back any benefit that was withheld because of the earnings test. So you are not getting penalized for working. But I want to be clear: You are still penalizing yourself by not holding out until age 70, when your benefit will be much larger.

FOCUS ON THE ODDS YOU MAY LIVE INTO YOUR 90'S

Okay, I know some of you are thinking, "But, Suze, I could die before I am 70 and then I will lose out." I understand where you are coming from, but I say this with love: You are looking at this completely wrong.

Your focus should be on making decisions today that will give you the most money if you live a very long life. Honestly, if you die at age 70, you don't have any retirement planning issues. Where it gets tricky is if you live a lot longer. You may worry about dying young. As your unofficial retirement planner, I worry how long you may live.

As I shared earlier, the odds a 65-year-old will still be alive at 90 are pretty good. Delaying so you can collect the higher benefit is like an insurance policy you will collect on if you have a long life.

I also know that some of you insist on framing this in terms of lifetime benefits, convinced that not starting early will leave money on the table. That shouldn't be your focus. Extra income for a long life is what should have your rapt attention.

But for those of you stuck on the lifetime benefits option, let me walk you through this scenario and why it may be a miscalculation.

Starting at 62 can seem like a good deal. You figure that the money you collect from 62 to 70 is money you will never be able to "make up" if you were to wait until age 70 to start. But that's where your plan can backfire. If you wait until age 70 to start collecting that much-higher benefit, by around age 82 you will have collected just as much in lifetime benefits as you would have if you started receiving the lower benefit at age 62. As I have already pointed out more than a few times, there is a good chance you will be alive into your 90s. So delaying would pay off.

Listen: My mom lived until she was 97, and her two sisters lived into their mid-90s. Given that both their parents had died in their 60s, the three sisters were convinced they would never make it to 80. Didn't quite happen the way they thought it would. I want you to consider the very likely possibility that you could live much longer than your parents.

DELAYING WILL HELP THE SURVIVING SPOUSE

If you are married, your strategy must be to plan for the highest earner to wait until age 70 to start collecting benefits. What is so important to understand is that when one of you dies, the surviving spouse is entitled to just one Social Security benefit: either keeping their own benefit or switching to the benefit of the deceased spouse. Having one benefit, not two, effectively reduces the income for the surviving spouse. If you have the high earner delay until age 70, you lock in the highest possible benefit for the surviving spouse. And just so you know, for a couple where both are 62 today, there is a 90% probability that one spouse will be alive in their early 80s.

CLAIMING IF YOU ARE DIVORCED

If you were married for at least 10 years, you may be eligible to collect a benefit based on an ex-spouse's earnings record. It doesn't matter if your ex is remarried; however, you can't be remarried. You also need to be at least 62, and the amount you would receive from the benefit tied to your ex's earnings record would have to be more than you would receive based on your own earnings record.

If you are contemplating divorce and are near the 10-year mark, you might want to consider holding out a bit longer.

SOCIAL SECURITY BENEFIT REDUCTION FOR CERTAIN PUBLIC-SECTOR RETIREES WITH PENSIONS

Some of you may have a pension from a government job where you and the employer did not pay into Social Security. If during your career, you also worked at a job where you did contribute to Social Security, you may run into a situation where your Social Security benefit is reduced because of the "non-covered" pension benefit. You can learn more about the Windfall Elimination Provision (WEP) at the Social Security website (www.ssa.gov/pubs /EN-05-10045.pdf), where you can also use a free online WEP calculator to estimate how your anticipated Social Security benefit could be impacted (www.ssa.gov/planners/retire/anyPiaWepjs04.html).

Try to wait, even if you stop working before 70.

By now you know I think it is so smart to keep working until you are at least 70. Being able to delay when you start Social Security is one of the biggest benefits to working through your 60s.

But I realize you may not be able to keep working. Maybe you have health issues. Maybe a recession eliminates your job. Maybe you are needed as a caregiver for family.

Even if you can't keep working through your 60s, I recommend you still try to delay starting Social Security. And that may be more possible than you think, if you have done a great job saving for retirement. Starting to tap your retirement savings in your 60s can be a better financial move than starting to collect Social Security.

Let's say you are 62 and your Social Security benefit if you claimed today would be $1,450 a month. If you wait until age 70, it would be about $2,550 a month.

You realize that the extra $1,100 a month would be fantastic to have once you turn 70, but, ooh, you really need that $1,450 now. I hear you. But I want you to see if you can pay yourself the $1,450 a month from savings and leave your Social Security benefit untouched until you reach 70.

Using this age 62 example, you would need to pay yourself $1,450 a month for eight years. That's nearly $140,000. If you have that in savings, I would consider tapping it each month. You can adjust each year for inflation if you really need to. I want you to use your savings and not start Social Security because of the difference in what both accounts can earn over those eight years. Money you have in safe savings is likely earning just 1% or 2%; if it's in a short-term bond fund, you are maybe earning 2.5% to 3%. That is a lot less than what you can earn by letting your Social Security benefit keep growing between age 62 and age 70. Remember: Your benefit will grow 76% between ages 62 and 70.

I want to be clear: This is not me giving you permission to stop working at 62 just because. Working for as long as possible is always going to be the best move. But if you find it is no longer practical to work at 62, or 65, or 67, I want you to know about this smart way to keep your Social Security intact and growing until age 70.

Don't worry about benefit cuts.

You likely are well aware that within the next 15 years, Social Security will run out of money to keep paying benefits at the current promised level. And the fearmongering—yes, it is fearmongering—that Social Security is going broke may understandably lead you to think you should start collecting ASAP, before Congress reduces your benefit.

I understand the concern, but I want to share some facts with you.

Fact 1: *Social Security is not going broke.* Going broke implies that no one will get paid a penny. That is not going to happen. Social Security has a cash-flow problem. The number of workers paying into the system through the payroll tax will not be enough to pay all the benefits promised to the legions of aging

Baby Boomers clamoring to collect. If Congress does nothing, benefits would have to be cut by about 25% to cover the shortfall beginning in 2035. Yes, 25% is a very big reduction, but it is not 100%.

Fact 2: *There are reasonable ways to fix the cash-flow gap.* For example, workers pay into the Social Security system through a payroll or self-employment tax. There is a cap on the annual income that is taxed. In 2020 that cap is $137,700. The system is designed to capture 90% of earnings in the U.S. However, because of income inequality, very high earners are paying an ever-smaller portion of their income into the system. Overall, the system is currently taxing less than 85% of our collective earned income. Adjusting the limit so it once again captures 90% of earned income could go a long way toward solving this shortfall.

Fact 3: *Changes will not likely have a big impact on anyone older than 50.* This isn't the first time Social Security needed tweaking. Nearly 40 years ago, a bipartisan commission tackled an impending cash-flow problem with a series of changes. Care was taken to phase in the changes to make sure no one was unduly impacted.

For example, one of the decisions was to raise the retirement age at which you are eligible for full benefits from 65 to its current maximum of 67, a change in large part based on longer life spans.

No one who was at least 46 years old at the time of the reform was affected. Their retirement age stayed at 65. The folks who now have an FRA of 67 were no older than 23 when their retirement age was increased from 65 to 67.

I think that is an important precedent to keep in mind. My eyes are wide-open to the fact that there is no saying what today's Washington might do. But with Social Security being the bedrock retirement income source for most Americans, I find it hard to conceive of Congress opting to greatly reduce the benefits of near-retirees.

I hope you see the incredible value of delaying when you start Social Security.

There are many angles you may want to consider. For example, married couples may want to explore different claiming options for the spouse with the lower benefit.

Given the many moving pieces to puzzle over, getting expert advice can be a valuable investment. As I explain in Chapter 8, you can hire reputable financial planners on a project or hourly basis; working through your Social Security strategy is a worthy project to pay for.

And if you're not sure you can wait until 70 because you don't want to keep working, a financial planner can also help you consider whether it makes sense to delay and start using other assets—your 401(k) and IRA, for example—in your 60s.

There are also online services created by wonky academics that will crunch your numbers and provide you with the best Social Security claiming strategy. You can learn more at Maximize My Social Security ($40: maximizemysocialsecurity.com) and

Social Security Solutions ($20 to $50: www.social securitysolutions.com/index.php).

Choose the safe pension payout option.

Since the 401(k) was launched in the early 1980s, many private sector employers have ditched offering old-fashioned pensions and only offer new employees the option of saving in a 401(k). But I know many of you have a pension from back in the day—the '70s and '80s—when they were more popular. And those of you who have worked in the public sector most likely have a pension.

There are many important decisions you must make with a traditional pension. The standard system is that you will receive a set monthly benefit based on a formula that factors in your salary and your years on the job. That part is set by the plan, with no decisions needed on your part. This arrangement is called an *annuity.*

If you are married, the choices begin. You can choose to have the payment be made only during your lifetime, or you can choose to have the payout continue if you die before your spouse. If you choose to continue payments for a surviving spouse, you will also need to decide how large you want that payout to be. That will affect the size of the payout you receive while you are alive.

Some pension plans now dangle an enticing-looking lump-sum option. Instead of an annuity that makes guaranteed monthly payouts, you get a one-time payout that you can roll over into an IRA that is then yours to manage. Some plans allow you to mix the two: You can take a partial lump sum and also receive a monthly check.

Here are strategies to consider with a pension:

Choose the monthly payout if you need the money for living costs.

A monthly pension benefit is guaranteed income. You know exactly what you are going to get each and every month. The stock market can be down 30% and your pension checks will not waver. That's exactly what you need if you expect to use the money to pay your essential living costs.

Learn more about how the federal government guarantees pension payments (up to certain limits) if your employer files for bankruptcy. Go to suzeorman.com/retirement.

Choose the 100% joint and survivor benefit if you are married.

With an annuity, which in essence is what you are choosing when you choose a payout from your company, you first must choose whether you want the payments to be "life only" or "joint and survivor." With a life-only policy, payments will stop when you die. Will that be a financial struggle if your spouse survives you? Remember: When a spouse dies, the survivor already faces an income drop, as there will be only one Social Security benefit.

If your spouse needs the income in order to live comfortably, hands down you must choose the joint and survivor option.

A POP-UP POSSIBILITY FOR MARRIED COUPLES

Some of you may have a pension that offers a "pop-up" provision.

This is an option worth considering for married couples, especially if the spouse of the pensioner has a health condition that suggests he or she may die first.

With a pop-up pension, the payout starts out based on it being a joint and survivor option: The payout will continue if the pensioner dies first. But in the event that the spouse dies first, the pensioner's monthly payment will then "pop up," meaning it will be recalculated as the life-only option, which will be a higher amount.

When you choose the joint and survivor option, you must also decide the size of the survivor's benefit. Typically you can choose for the survivor's benefit to be 100%, 75%, or 50% of the benefit while you are alive.

The monthly benefit while you are alive will be higher if you choose life only. It will be higher if you choose the 50% survivor benefit rather than the 75% benefit. And the 75% benefit will be higher than the 100% benefit.

It can be very tempting to take a higher benefit today, but please do not make this mistake. The highest benefit today is not what matters. If your spouse is healthy, I strongly believe you should choose the 100% option no matter what.

If your spouse has a serious health condition that you expect to shorten their life, then you may want to consider a lower percentage if you expect within a few years you will be the surviving spouse. But please be very, very careful here. You want to make sure you understand the consequence of things playing out differently than planned. If you die first, will your spouse have enough income to live comfortably?

For married couples, retirement planning is all about doing everything you can to ensure the smoothest financial situation for the surviving spouse. My strong recommendation, again, is that you choose the 100% payout option if there is any chance your spouse will survive you.

DON'T CHOOSE THE LIFE-ONLY OPTION WITH THE INTENTION OF BUYING TERM LIFE INSURANCE

Way too often married couples come to me with a pension strategy someone has recommended that supposedly shows it is a better deal to choose the life-only option and then protect the spouse by buying life insurance. This is not smart at all.

Look, I get the appeal. If you chose life only, you will indeed get a higher monthly payment than if you opt for a pension with a 100% joint and survivor payout. So you think you'll buy a term insurance policy to protect the surviving spouse in the event the spouse with the pension dies first. Given that term insurance is relatively inexpensive, you think you will come out ahead if you take the higher life-only payout and use a small portion of that to cover the term insurance.

But there is a huge flaw in this strategy. As much as I love term insurance, it is the wrong type of insurance for this situation. It is only good for a set number of years—the term—so what happens if you die after the term insurance expires? Your spouse will not have an insurance policy to fall back on. You need a whole-life permanent insurance policy if you are going to opt for a pension that will not leave any benefit for your spouse. And the premium cost of a whole-life policy is a lot more than for a term life policy. In most instances you will find that the premium for a whole-life policy will cost you more than the extra payout you are getting from a life-only pension. You are likely going to be better off choosing the lower 100% joint and survivor benefit on your pension and avoiding the need for any life insurance.

Don't take a lump sum payout and then buy an annuity.

Please do not listen to anyone who tells you to take the lump-sum option, roll it into an IRA, and then use the money to buy an annuity. This makes me nuts. The annuity you will be offered by your pension is a better deal than buying one on your own.

When you buy an annuity on your own, there will be a commission to pay . . . to the person insisting this is a fabulous idea.

And do not fall for slick sales presentations showing that there are better annuities than the one you will get inside your pension. If you are relying on this income to cover your living costs in retirement, the straightforward annuity offered by your pension is exactly what you want. It is a plain-vanilla income annuity: guaranteed income for life at a low cost. Anything being sold to you with the promise of better outcomes has two potential problems: Those "better" outcomes won't be guaranteed, and the person selling it is likely collecting a fee.

A lump sum can make sense if you don't need to cover retirement living costs.

As we will cover in Chapter 6, a smart income strategy is to make sure you can pay all your basic living costs from guaranteed income sources. Social Security is a guaranteed income source. So too is a monthly pension payment. If you have saved for retirement in a traditional 401(k), 403(b), or IRA, you will have to take Required Minimum Distributions (RMDs) by the following April 1 once you turn 70½ if born on or before 6/30/49, or 72 if born after. The RMD is a percentage of your account assets based on your age. (More on RMDs in Chapter 6). Assuming a portion of those accounts is invested in stocks, your RMD is not guaranteed income. Any year when stocks fall in value, your RMD will fall. Those RMDs will generate income; we just don't know for sure how much.

If you add up all these income sources and it is more than you need to cover your retirement living costs, then you may not need to take your pension as an annuity. Or if you are married and you both have pensions, you might determine that one annuitized pension in the family is enough.

Taking the lump sum is something to consider if you anticipate not needing the money and wanting to leave an inheritance. But as I explain next, you would also be taking on a very big responsibility that can backfire.

A lump sum is riskier than an annuity.

This bears repeating: A monthly pension payout is guaranteed income. There will be nothing guaranteed if you instead take a lump sum and then invest the money. Even if you invest in cash and bonds, you take on some risk; if interest rates decline, so too will your income. And if your intention is to invest a portion of your lump-sum payout in stocks, you will be taking on an even greater risk.

That may be a risk worth taking; if you are sure you don't need the money, and this is about building a legacy for your heirs, taking a lump sum and investing it has merit. But I do not recommend this strategy if your intention is to invest the money to pay for your living costs. Sticking with the guaranteed monthly annuity payout the pension offers is wiser.

There's another risk I want you to consider. An investment portfolio requires you stay on top of things: notably, rebalancing and making sure you take your RMDs. (If you do not take the correct RMD, there will be a 50% penalty tax on what you should have withdrawn.) From time to time, you will have to reassess whether your investments are still best in class. As you age that can be something you don't want to do. And let's be honest: It may be something you are not capable of doing as well at 88 as you can at 68. Dementia, Alzheimer's, or the cognitive decline that comes with age should be a consideration in your retirement planning. A monthly pension payment is a sneaky, smart way to avoid this risk down the line. There's nothing to manage. There's no way a bad actor can get access to the money. Elder financial abuse is a very sad but very real issue.

A partial lump sum may be a good compromise.

Ask your employer if partial lump sums are allowed. The money you take as a lump sum is yours to manage, but you will also leave behind some money that will be annuitized, creating a guaranteed monthly income stream.

If you aren't able (or willing) to keep working through your 60s, a partial lump sum might be money you can tap before you are 70 in lieu of starting Social Security.

Because of the lump sum, your monthly pension payout will be less than if you chose the annuity for the entire amount, but that may be the right trade-off for your circumstances: some guaranteed income, some money to invest or spend.

If you take the lump sum, make sure you do what is called a *custodian to custodian transfer* (discussed earlier in this chapter) in which your funds are transferred directly to your rollover account. Do not ask for your lump sum to be direct-deposited into your personal bank account. If you do not follow certain guidelines, this could trigger a very big tax bill that could, in turn, bump you into a higher tax bracket. And as we will discuss in a moment, Medicare charges higher Part B premiums for higher-income individuals.

Enroll in Medicare and supplemental coverage.

Medicare is a vital piece of your retirement financial plan that will provide broad coverage for your health care needs.

But I want to dispel an all-too-common notion that once you enroll in Medicare, you don't have to worry about your health care expenses.

In fact, as expansive as the program is, it is not in any way free. There is a basic monthly premium for one part of Medicare that then pays 80% of your costs. You are responsible for the other 20%. Nor are prescription drugs part of the basic coverage; you have to pay extra for that coverage, and depending on the medications you need, you may still have co-pays for certain medications. You will also likely want to purchase additional coverage that goes beyond Medicare basics.

On average, if you bunch together all the premiums/deductibles/co-pays, etc., you will pay for about 30% of your retirement health care costs. The

Employee Benefit Research Institute calculated that in 2019, a 65-year-old man with typical prescription drug needs throughout retirement might require more than $140,000 to have a high probability that he could cover his expected out-of-pocket health care costs. A 65-year-old woman would need more than $160,000 to cover her retirement health care costs.

And I want to be clear: None of this includes long-term care costs. Medicare doesn't cover those at all, and pays for skilled nursing home care for a relatively short number of days. (If that just gave you pause, I invite you to reread what I had to say about Health Savings Accounts and long-term care insurance in Chapter 3.)

Given what's at stake, I know you will want to make sure you make smart choices about your retirement health care coverage.

And you will have multiple choices. Medicare is not a single program: It is a series of different programs; some are mandatory, some optional.

There is no single best approach that is right for everyone. If you want full freedom to seek out any doctor, you will likely prefer an option called *Original Medicare* more than another option, called *Medicare Advantage*, which typically pays for coverage only when you use in-network doctors.

You also have to decide how you want to purchase insurance for prescription drugs. If you opt for a Medicare Advantage plan, prescription drug coverage is typically included. But if you enroll in an Original Medicare plan, you will need to purchase a separate Medicare Part D insurance policy to provide coverage for prescription drugs.

WHEN TO ENROLL

Before we explore all those options in detail, I want to make sure you are clear on when you need to enroll in Medicare. *Need* is what I said. This is not something you take care of when you feel like it. There are penalties and potential denial of coverage if you don't enroll at the correct time.

You become eligible for Medicare at age 65, but when you need to sign up for Medicare depends on your work situation at age 65.

Not Working at 65

If you have stopped working, it is imperative to enroll at age 65.

If you have stopped working but remain on an employer's health insurance plan, at 65 you also need to enroll in Medicare. Even if you have "retiree" benefits, they typically only cover costs *after* Medicare.

Failure to hit the 65 deadline will trigger a penalty being tacked onto the monthly premium you pay for Medicare Part B coverage (more on this below). The penalty is 10% of the premium cost for every 12-month period you are without Medicare Part B coverage. Even once you are enrolled, the extra penalty added to your premium will not be removed. You are stuck with the extra cost for life.

Thankfully, you have a wide, seven-month window to sign up around your 65th birthday: You can enroll anytime in the three months before your birthday month, and up to three months after your birthday month.

If you are collecting your Social Security retirement benefit before you are 65, you will automatically be enrolled and your monthly premium costs will be deducted from your Social Security benefit. But I sure hope that after hearing me out on waiting until age 70 to start your Social Security benefit, you aren't collecting it at 65. In that case, you will need to sign up on your own. Keep reading.

Still Working at 65 with Health Insurance Coverage

If you are still working at a job that provides health insurance, or you are covered by a spouse's plan, you may continue to rely on that coverage and delay signing up for Medicare. But please be very careful here: Only companies with at least 20 employees are required to continue coverage for workers once they turn 65.

Once you stop work or the workplace coverage ends, you have an eight-month grace period to get signed up for Medicare and avoid the 10% penalty.

If you intend to keep working past 65 and you have workplace insurance, before your birthday make an appointment to sit down with HR and understand what your options are.

And be careful if you think it would be wise to "play it safe" and enroll in Medicare even if you are still covered through work. As I explain later in this section, when you enroll in Medicare, you have the option of buying supplemental insurance to cover expenses that Medicare doesn't pay for. These policies are called *Medigap insurance.*

If you sign up for a Medigap policy within six months of signing up for Medicare, your Medigap premium will not be impacted by any pre-existing conditions. After that six-month window, insurers can charge anyone signing up for Medigap coverage more, or deny coverage.

What I want you to avoid is signing up for Medicare when you still have workplace insurance but not signing up for Medigap insurance because you figure you don't need that "yet" given your workplace coverage. If you continue to have workplace coverage, it is likely far safer and smarter to delay signing up for Medicare (and Medigap) until you are no longer covered by an employer plan.

If sometime between age 65 and 70 (when you start receiving Social Security benefits), you need to start Medicare, you can you can do it online at the Social Security website (www.ssa.gov/benefits/medicare).

YOUR MEDICARE OPTIONS

Let's start with a review of the various elements of Medicare and supplemental health care coverage. For married couples it's important to understand that there is no coverage for you as a couple. You both must enroll in your own individual plans.

Medicare Part A

This is for in-hospital coverage, hospice care, and skilled nursing care (for a limited number of days). When you enroll in Medicare, this coverage is provided without any monthly premium cost if you paid into the Medicare fund for at least 10 years. If you worked at least that long and your paycheck included FICA deductions, you're all set. There is a deductible when you use any services under Part A. The standard deductible in 2020 is $1,408. (If you buy supplemental insurance, it will likely cover this cost.)

Medicare Part B

This covers your general care when you are not hospitalized: doctor appointments, tests, outpatient procedures. Typically, Medicare pays for 80% of these bills. If you purchase a Medicare Advantage or Medigap supplemental policy (details below), those policies will cover your 20% coinsurance cost.

There is a monthly premium for Part B coverage. In 2020 the base premium is $144.60 a month for individuals with incomes below $87,000 and married couples filing a joint tax return with incomes below $174,000. Higher-income households pay more. In 2020 the maximum Part B monthly premium is $491.60 per person.

Once you are receiving your Social Security benefit, the premium is automatically deducted from your payment each month. Before then, you will need to pay Medicare directly. When you enroll, you will receive billing information.

Medicare Part A and Medicare Part B are referred to as *Original Medicare.*

Medicare Part C

Also called *Medicare Advantage.* A Medicare Advantage plan is a private policy you buy from an insurance company that offers you all-in-one coverage. A Medicare Advantage plan offers the same coverage as Medicare Part A and Part B, and it will typically include Part D prescription drug coverage as well.

Many Medicare Advantage plans also offer coverage for dental, vision, and hearing, though there is wide variance among plans in what is actually covered. And Medicare Advantage plans are beginning to provide LTC benefits, but the coverage so far is meager.

That is a lot of coverage, and convenience, often at an affordable price. The average Medicare Advantage premium in 2020 is aroudnd $36 a month, in addition to the Part B premium.

That said, there are potential drawbacks to consider.

Medicare Advantage plans typically operate like Health Maintenance Organization (HMOs): You are restricted to doctors within your plan's network, and you typically need to get pre-approval for consultations and treatment. Some are PPOs; your coverage is restricted to in-network doctors, and if you want to see someone out of network, you will pay more. If you want to see specific doctors, you need to check that they are part of a Medicare Advantage plan you are considering.

Moreover, the insurers that offer Medicare Advantage plans often deny treatments.

Medicare Advantage plans are overseen by the federal agency that runs the Medicare program. Each insurer is paid a fixed fee by the government to provide coverage. That seems to lead some insurers to exert a heavy hand in denying medical procedures/care to keep their costs lower.

A 2018 report from the U.S. Department of Health and Human Services said that more than half of Medicare Advantage plans were cited for improperly denying coverage to enrollees. A sign that those denials were sketchy is that 75% of people denied coverage who knew enough to keep pushing for coverage eventually had their treatment request approved.

Medicare Part D

If you choose to enroll in Original Medicare, then you need to be aware that prescription drug coverage is not part of your standard coverage. A Part D plan provides prescription drug coverage. The monthly premium typically runs $30 to $40 a month.

You will have a choice of plans offered in your region. Please don't shop on premium alone. You want to dive into the coverage details and confirm that any medications you already take will cost you nothing (preferred generic versions of many popular medications) or a reasonable co-pay. At the Medicare website, you can use the Basic search option for the Medicare Plan Finder to search for Part D plans in your area that offer the lowest out-of-pocket costs for the drugs you take (www.medicare.gov/plan-compare). Once you identify a plan you like, call or e-mail the plan and confirm the current out-of-pocket costs of the drugs you take; the Medicare Plan Finder is a great tool, but you need to be extra sure how the plan works before you sign on.

Medigap Insurance

If you opt for Original Medicare, you will want to consider purchasing a supplemental policy, called *Medigap* coverage. A Medigap policy can cover the cost of your co-pays and deductibles from Medicare Parts A and B. To have insurance for prescription drugs, you will need to purchase a separate Medicare Part D policy. (In the past, Medigap policies provided drug coverage, but since Part D was launched, new Medigap enrollees must get that coverage apart from a Medigap policy.)

There are different types of Medigap policies, offering different levels of coverage. Plans vary by region. The Medicare Plan Finder can help you find Medigap and Medicare Advantage plans in your area, and compare their coverages (www.medicare.gov /find-a-plan/questions/home.aspx).

I want to repeat something I shared earlier: If you are going to sign up for a Medigap policy, please make sure you do so when you enroll in Medicare. If you pair the two moves, you must be offered a Medigap policy regardless of any pre-existing conditions and at the same price as all other enrollees. If you enroll in Medicare at age 65, you have six months from the month of your birthday to also enroll in Medigap.

If you are still working at 65 and have coverage through your employer, you can delay enrolling in Medicare until that coverage stops or you stop working. At that point you have up to eight months to get enrolled in Medicare. And if you intend to purchase Medigap insurance, you will want to enroll within that same window to avoid any extra charges or coverage denial for pre-existing conditions.

HEAD ONLINE TO SHOP AROUND

Medicare's Medicare Plan Finder is a free website that will show you Medicare plans in your region and allows you to compare plans (www .medicare.gov/plan-compare). There are also state health insurance programs (SHIPs) that can help you sort through your options (www.ship tacenter .org). The Medicare Interactive tool run by the non-profit Medicare Rights Center is a good resource for detailed information on plans and rules (www .medicareinteractive.org).

COMMIT TO AN ANNUAL PLAN CHECKUP

Once a year, from October 15 to Dec 7, you can switch your Medicare plans during Open Enrollment season.

Most people don't bother checking to see if their existing plans are still a smart choice. That can be a costly mistake, as plans can and will change what they cover and what they charge.

Your current plan will send you information about any changes for the coming year. Read it. And then head back to the Medicare Plan Finder to compare your plan to others.

I want you to pay particular attention to the price tier for drugs you take. Medicare Advantage and Medicare Part D drug plans offer different types of coverage for different drugs. Generic versions of mainstream drugs often require no co-pay, or a small co-pay of $10 or so. But some drugs are in "non-preferred" tiers and can cost you plenty.

What you need to stay on top of is that each year the plans can change these so-called "formularies." A prescription that didn't have a co-pay last year might cost you $20 or $50 or more every time you fill it next year. At the extreme, certain high-cost drugs can be dropped from the plan completely, which would require you to pay the full cost.

And what's crazy is that plans offered in your region can charge widely different co-pays for the same drug. The difference could be $1,000 or more depending on the drug, according to a 2019 survey by the Senior Citizens League.

Investing some time in researching your best options for the coming year is well worth it. Again, you can use Medicare's Medicare Plan Finder to compare coverage and cost for the coming year (www.medicare .gov/plan-compare). There are also state health insurance programs (SHIPs) that can help you sort through your options (www.shiptacenter.org).

Be flexible if a bear market hits in early retirement.

At this stage of your investing life, you are no stranger to bear markets. There have been seven times since 1970 when the S&P 500 Index fell at least 20%. I hope you have learned that patience pays off. It typically takes just a few years for stocks to recover bear-market losses. Even with two severe bear markets this century, $10,000 invested in the S&P 500 was worth $30,000 in late 2019. If you had that $10,000 sitting in the bank, it would have grown to about $14,000.

The odds of you running into a few more bear markets during a retirement that may last 25 to 30 years are pretty high. No matter how experienced you are with bear markets, there is a new risk you need to be aware of as you are nearing retirement and during the early years of retirement.

A bear market that hits in the first five years or so of retirement increases the chance that your investment portfolio might not last as long as you need it to. When you make withdrawals in the early years of retirement from a portfolio that is already down because of bear-market losses, you are taking an extra bite out of a pot of money you need to support you for another 20 or more years.

Granted, you can't control when a bear market hits, but you have control over how you respond if there is a big stock slide near when your retirement starts, or in the first few years.

Not retired yet? Good. Keep working.

If in the year or two before you intend to retire, a bear market hits, consider delaying your retirement. Continuing to work means you won't need to start making withdrawals when your stock portfolio is down.

I realize staying full time may not be practical for everyone. But please consider what work you might be able to keep doing to give your portfolio time to recover. Even if you shift to a part-time job, that can make it possible to make smaller withdrawals from your investment accounts.

Stick with stocks.

Selling stocks after they have fallen is selling too late. And it creates another problem because you will have a very hard time knowing when to get back into stocks. When you attempt to time the market, you need to be right twice: when to sell and when to buy again. No one is good at this.

That said, before you retire you should have a clear strategy for how much of your investment portfolio is invested in stocks. I cover this in detail in Chapter 7. Once you have your strategy in place, you should not sell stocks during a bear market.

Build a bear-market income strategy.

Now is the time to put a plan in place that will make it possible to stay invested in stocks in a bear market and give your stock portfolio the time it needs to recover. There are two main strategies to consider:

Cover your essential living costs with guaranteed income. Cash in the bank is guaranteed income. Social Security is guaranteed income. A pension annuity is guaranteed income. You can also create your own pension by buying an income annuity. (Yes, some annuities are awful. Income annuities can be good annuities. More on this in Chapter 6.)

If you have your living costs covered by guaranteed income, you won't need to touch your stocks in a bear market. And I think you might sleep a lot better, right?

If you plan to rely on money in the bank to cover your living expenses in a bear market, I would recommend you have at least two years of living expenses set aside for bear market living expenses. (This is in addition to your emergency fund.) That's typically enough time for your investment portfolio to recover. But if you feel better with three years, that's fine. Just keep in mind that there can be a downside to playing it too safe: Money invested in cash likely will not grow at a rate that keeps pace with inflation. And as I explain in Chapter 7, that's a risk you need to work around. Having some money in cash is smart. But you don't want all of it in cash.

Take the money out of the bond side of your portfolio. In a bear market, withdrawals you make from investment accounts should be taken out of your bond holdings. Do. Not. Touch. Your. Stocks.

Bear markets are exactly the reason you own bonds. Heading into retirement, the best types of bonds to own are U.S. Treasuries. They are the bonds that hold up best in bear markets. When the S&P 500 stock index lost 55% during the 2007 to 2009 bear market, a conservative portfolio of Treasury bonds gained more than 15%. Yes, I said *gained*.

In Chapter 7 we will discuss how to land on a stock/bond allocation strategy that feels right to you. For most of you, a bond allocation of between 40% and 50% or so when you are in your 60s should strike the right balance and give you plenty to draw on during a bear market.

You know what else will get you through a bear market? Common sense! If you rein in your spending, you will need to tap less money during a bear market. Maybe you delay a big trip. Or spend a bit less on eating out or nights on the town. Or remind yourself that what you spend on gifts is not a reflection of your love. Take a spin through your monthly spending and challenge yourself to cut your nonessential costs by at least 20%—something I recommend whether you are 35 or 75.

YOUR ULTIMATE RETIREMENT CHECKLIST

❑ Focus your retirement plan on living until *at least* age 95.

❑ Decide whether a 401(k) rollover to an IRA account makes sense.

❑ Make it your goal to wait until age 70 to start receiving your Social Security retirement benefit.

❑ Be very careful if you are tempted to take a lump-sum payout from a pension.

❑ Choose the 100% joint and survivor option for a pension if you are married and your spouse is in good health.

❑ Enroll in Medicare at 65 (if you don't have coverage at work) and consider purchasing supplemental Medicare coverage.

❑ Review your Medicare choices every year.

❑ Set a plan for how you will handle a bear market in your 60s.

CHAPTER 6:

HOW TO PAY YOURSELF IN RETIREMENT (AND NOT RUN OUT OF MONEY)

As you near retirement, you must take on a new and demanding job: figuring out how to convert your savings into a reliable stream of income that can support you through a long retirement.

After decades of earning income and saving for retirement, you need to shift gears and get comfortable spending what you have saved. Plus, you'll have to figure out a strategy that will give you the income you need from your first month of retirement all the way through to your 90s.

It's not just your investment accounts you'll have to wrestle with. As I have already mentioned, deciding when to start taking your Social Security benefit will have a huge impact on your retirement income. And for those of you with a pension, there is a series of decisions you need to carefully consider.

I know this can cause a good deal of retirement planning anxiety. But there is no need to be nervous or intimidated. I want you to understand that you have all sorts of life experience in the very skills you need in order to tackle this latest project.

If you are a cook who enjoys digging into an involved recipe, you know that the trick is in combining different ingredients in just the right proportions so that they come together to create something delicious.

If you are a parent, you have juggled, planned, and rolled with the punches every day, for years.

If you are blessed with the rare skill of being able to easily assemble IKEA furniture, you know how to literally put the pieces together to create a useful and pleasing object.

What does this have to do with retirement? Plenty! Your experience in working through projects—no matter what the specific task may be—is exactly what you need now to help you figure out how best to pay yourself a steady and reliable stream of income in retirement. Please listen to me: You don't need to learn a new skill. You need to apply skills you have been using for years in a new way—paying yourself in retirement.

The key to this challenge bears repeating: *steady and reliable income. Steady* refers to having at least the income you need to cover all your living expenses each and every month, even when the stock market is down. *Reliable* means your plan will not burn through your money too quickly. As I have already explained, I think at a minimum you should plan on living to age 95; my best advice is to build your retirement income plan as if you will still be alive at 100.

The decisions you make today about how to generate steady and reliable income throughout your retirement are what will allow you to actually enjoy retirement. Taking the time up-front to carefully consider how best to generate the income you need at a pace that will last you decades will be a huge emotional relief. This planning is what will make it possible to not worry about money and to enjoy retirement. And that's what you've been working so hard for, right?

IT'S PERSONAL

Over the years I have been helping people with retirement planning, I've found that there is no one plan that is right for everyone. As strongly as I believe that waiting until you are 70 to claim Social Security is one of the smartest retirement income decisions you can make, I know some of you will insist on starting earlier. Many of you will be comfortable keeping 50% or so of your investment accounts in stocks. For others, having that much in stocks will set off stress alarms and likely cause you to make costly emotional moves in a bear market.

Just about the worst retirement outcome I can imagine is that you push yourself to make choices that you aren't comfortable with, and then you spend your retirement years anxious and worried about money.

That is the opposite of why I wrote this book. The ultimate retirement is all about focusing on the people and the activities that bring you happiness and fulfillment. That is only possible if you free your mind from money worries.

The strategy you land on may incorporate everything I recommend in these pages, or you may make adjustments that work for you. You must make the right decision for you—taking ownership is a big step toward peace of mind. My job is to make sure you have the knowledge to make an informed decision that carefully considers the consequences of the choices you make.

If after considering all the options you feel a bit unsure about how to proceed, this is where a reputable financial advisor can be incredibly helpful. Financial planners specialize in understanding all the moving pieces and how they interact. A good advisor does more than crunch the numbers and tell you what to do. The good ones listen, and they understand what is easy for you to implement and what will make you fearful and anxious. A good plan will address both your money and your mind-set. Good financial planners know that the best plan is the one you will be comfortable sticking with. They will encourage you to consider the best financial strategies, and then adapt as needed to make sure you are comfortable with and committed to your plan.

To be clear, even the most fantastic certified financial planner or advisor isn't a magician. For many of you, there may be important trade-offs to consider. Having a steady, reliable income stream that covers your living costs may involve rethinking staying in your current home or the payoff if you can keep working for a few more years. There are many ways you can get to a steady and reliable income. Having a pro work through all the moving parts and help you craft a plan can be a smart investment. In Chapter 8 I discuss how to find a financial advisor whom you can trust.

THE MOVES TO MAKE TO PAY YOURSELF IN RETIREMENT (AND NOT RUN OUT OF MONEY)

- Know your expenses.

- Calculate your reliable income sources.

- Pay your fixed living expenses from guaranteed income.

- Keep two years of living expenses in cash.

- Hatch an RMD plan.

- Plan to spend no more than 3% of your portfolio in the first year of retirement.

Know your expenses.

This seems so basic, but my experience is that many of you don't know what you really spend each month. You just sort of wing it. When I sit down with people to go over their spending, they typically underestimate their actual spending by $500 or more a month.

You have a pretty good idea of the recurring expenses: what you spend on groceries, the mortgage/rent, utilities, etc. But you forget to add in the many expenses you face less often. All your insurance premiums. Vacations. Gifts. All that less-routine spending adds up!

Now, some good news is that in retirement a few expenses disappear. No more saving for retirement! No more contributing your share of the Social Security and Medicare payroll tax (that's the FICA line on your pay stub). No more commuting.

But you may have new expenses. Especially in the early years of retirement, it is common to want to travel more, for example. I see expenses increase in the case of surviving spouses too. I call it the loneliness factor. You don't like eating alone, so you go out to eat more, and you treat. You go to visit the kids more. You take more trips. I just want you to factor in all these probabilities so that, in fact, you really get your retirement income stream and expenses correct.

> *Learn more.* At my website I have a free expense calculator that will help you figure out a realistic picture of what your spending will look like in retirement. Go to suzeorman .com/retirement.

Calculate your reliable income sources.

This is obviously a very important calculation, and one that is not easy to figure out. As we covered in the previous chapter, you have options with Social Security and a pension, if you have a pension, that will determine the income you will receive from both. Another important consideration is that your Social Security benefit will grow with inflation, yet it is rare for pensions to include inflation adjustments.

And those are the easy pieces of your income plan!

Figuring out the income you can generate from your retirement investments accounts—401(k)s and IRAs—is the tricky part. You need to make assumptions about the potential growth rate for your accounts, which will depend on the mix of stocks and bonds you decide works best for you. Taxes are going to take a big bite out of withdrawals from traditional retirement accounts, so that's another issue to work through.

Those retirement accounts will require you to begin making annual Required Minimum Distributions (RMDs) by the following April 1 once you turn 70½ if born on or before 6/30/49, or 72 if born after that date. As I will explain later in this chapter, I think many of you may want to consider not spending all of your annual RMDs. Once you take the RMD and pay the tax—which, as I noted, is why the federal government is forcing you to take the RMD—you may find that reinvesting some of that money will help you keep supporting yourself well into your 90s.

This is where sitting down with a financial planner can be very smart. A good planner will have the software that can run all sorts of careful calculations based on a variety of scenarios that will help you develop a clear picture of what your after-tax income can be in retirement.

> *Learn more.* At my website the free Income/Expense calculator will help you estimate what your reliable monthly income will be. That can help you start thinking through your options. Go to suzeorman.com /retirement.

That said, you must be in control of your decisions, and that means taking some time to understand the mechanics of building a reliable income stream.

There are three building blocks to your retirement income:

1. Social Security
2. Pension income (if you are eligible)
3. Income from your investments

We have already walked through why I think the highest earner in a household should consider waiting until age 70 to start receiving Social Security; for those of you who are married and have a pension, I made my case for choosing the 100% joint and survivor benefit.

I want to stress (again) that for those of you who are married, your planning today must take into account how monthly income will change when one of you dies. A surviving spouse can collect one Social Security benefit, not two. Pension payouts can also be lower once a spouse dies; in some cases the surviving spouse may not get any pension payout.

The safest way to plan is to make sure your household's living expenses—needs, not wants—are covered by a steady stream of income not only while both of you are alive but after the death of one of you. Not an easy topic to think about, but it is reality.

We will cover how much income you can safely pull from your investment accounts in detail later in this chapter. Here's a preview: Many of you may be familiar with the strategy that says if your money is split between stocks and bonds, you can withdraw 4% of the balance in the first year of retirement and adjust that for inflation each subsequent year, and your money should last you for at least 30 years. For reasons I will explain later, I think it is smart for anyone retiring soon to reduce their first-year spending to 3% of their portfolio balance.

The free Income/Expense Calculator at my website will help you begin to understand your potential income. If your income is not nearly enough to cover your expenses, don't panic. You have options. You have control. You must stand in your truth, take responsibility, and make the right choices. As we have already covered in earlier chapters, working longer, curbing your spending, and considering a home move to reduce your living expenses will all help you bring your expenses and income into line.

What I will never agree to is a decision to just give up and decide you will spend more of your investment portfolio early in your retirement, or run up big credit card balances you never expect to pay off. That's not exactly a warrior move, is it?

Lately I have been getting a lot of letters from adult children asking what they can do to get their retired parents to understand that they cannot keep spending down the money in their retirement accounts at their current pace. I have to tell you, I find this very sad. The children—who are in their 30s, 40s, and 50s— are worried because they themselves do not have the money to take care of their parents. Their parents have gotten into a difficult, unsustainable situation because they did not figure out, before they retired, their true income versus expenses.

I am asking you to stand in your truth now. If you don't have a reliable income stream that can support you for a long life, then you are probably going to make your life and your kids' lives more difficult. I can't imagine that is what you would ever intend.

Pay your fixed living expenses from guaranteed income.

A retirement income strategy can sometimes feel like being pulled in two opposing directions. You want to know you will have the money you need to take care of yourself. That's an argument for safe investments. But all the longevity statistics we have discussed make a clear case that over a multi-decade retire- ment, inflation can be a problem. That's an argument for owning some stocks, which have the best chance of generating inflation-beating gains. But that means signing on for living through bear markets, which can be harder to weather emotionally in retirement.

I want you to give serious consideration to a strat- egy that can give you the stability so many of you crave, and the confidence to own some stocks too.

The stability you want is knowing you can pay your essential living costs no matter what. Period.

Full stop. If the markets are cratering, you want to know you've got income coming that is steady and secure and will allow you to cover your living costs. I hear you.

As I said before, there are a few types of retirement income sources that offer guaranteed income.

1. Social Security
2. A pension
3. An income annuity you purchase

Guaranteed means that these are income sources that have nothing to do with the stock or bond markets. What you receive each month is set. It will not go up or down with market changes. The world can be going crazy around you, and those direct deposit payments will just keep on coming, every month.

If it is help-me-sleep-at-night stability you want, your goal should be to cover all your essential living expenses from these guaranteed income sources.

If Social Security (and a pension, if you have one) don't give you enough to cover your essential bills, you can buy an investment that works like a pension to cover the gap.

An income annuity can be a smart way to round out your guaranteed income needs.

Let's get something straight: There are some god-awful annuities that are sold by insurance agents who care more about the big commissions they earn on those sales than what is best for the client.

I understand if you are extremely skeptical about annuities. I actually am pleased if you're cringing at the thought; it means you are aware of the potential pitfalls.

I hear you loud and clear. I agree with you 100%.

Do you honestly think I would ever steer you into anything that was bad for you? I am recommending one and only one type of annuity: an income annuity.

In the next section I will tell you everything you need to know about income annuities. For now, I just want you to know that if after adding up your Social Security benefit, and perhaps a pension, you are short on having the guaranteed income you need, purchasing an income annuity is an option that can close your guaranteed income gap.

I also need you to consider the other way to close your guaranteed income gap: Reduce your living costs.

If your gap is small, you may be able to close it with a few targeted trims. Maybe a slightly lower travel budget or reining in your spending on your adult kids . . . and their kids. Or reducing your entertainment budget a bit.

If there is a large gap, I want you to circle back to Chapter 4. There is no greater way to save than to reconsider where you will live in retirement. And who you will live with.

There is an additional payoff to the guaranteed income strategy. It should give you the confidence to be able to invest in stocks for the long term. You know your guaranteed income has your back: Those checks will keep coming, steady and reliable. That should make it easier to keep some of your investment portfolio in stocks to help you keep pace with inflation over the years.

Consider an income annuity to generate the guaranteed income you want.

There is one type of annuity that is a good deal for retirees. Income annuities.

Got it? Income annuities.

Not variable annuities. Not fixed indexed annuities. Income annuities. Period.

An income annuity, which is sometimes referred to as a *fixed income annuity*, is a personal pension you create for yourself. You give money to an insurance company—a lump sum is typical prior to retirement—and the insurance company then agrees to send you a locked-in payment every month once your annuity starts.

The amount you receive is based on a few main factors:

- Your age
- How long the payments will continue; you can choose a lifetime payment, or payments for a specific period, say, 10 or 20 years
- Whether payments will continue for a surviving spouse or partner
- Current interest rates when you purchase the annuity
- Whether you want your benefit to increase with inflation each year

For guaranteed income, I think you will want to focus on a lifetime payout. If you are married, you should consider an annuity that will continue at the same level for the surviving spouse.

Income annuities come in two basic flavors:

- **Immediate income annuities.** You pay your one-time premium to the insurance company, and payments start, well, immediately.

- **Deferred income annuities.** You buy the annuity today, but don't start the payouts until a set period of time, such as 5 years or 10 years. During the period before you start, the premium you paid will earn a fixed rate of return.

If you are looking to create more guaranteed income for your retirement right now, the immediate income annuity will make sense. If you are eager to lock in your guaranteed income plan before you retire, a deferred income annuity is worth considering.

Focus on the peace of mind you are buying.

Survey after survey finds near unanimous hunger for guaranteed income in retirement. No surprise there. But when a solution is offered—income annuities—let's just say interest is lacking.

The deserved bad rap of the "other" types of annuities may be partly to blame.

But the bigger issue is often about the loss of control. You are concerned that if you buy an income annuity, the money you pay the insurer is no longer yours, and you focus on the risk that you may die before the total payments you have received are at least equal to the premium you paid the insurer.

That perspective overlooks the fact that an annuity is not merely an investment. It is also an insurance policy. And insurance is about protecting yourself, not solely making a great investment.

You buy home insurance just in case. You buy auto insurance hoping you will never need to make a claim. You did not buy term life insurance when you were younger with the hope it would be used, right?

Yet when it comes to buying retirement protection—protection against living a long time and your savings not being able to support you—your back bristles.

I understand we are talking big sums of money. For example, in late 2019 a 70-year-old woman who wants $1,000 in guaranteed monthly income for the rest of her life would need to spend nearly $200,000 to purchase an income annuity that would deliver her that monthly peace of mind. For a 70-year-old male married to a 67-year-old woman, locking in $1,000 a month until the surviving spouse dies would cost around $220,000.

But I encourage you to reframe your focus just a bit and think about what problems can be solved with an income annuity.

If you place a high value on having guaranteed income, you should seriously consider adding an income annuity to complement your Social Security. If you place a high value on making sure your spouse will have ample guaranteed income if you die first, why wouldn't you consider adding an income annuity? If only one of you is involved in handling your investments, an income annuity will be a great gift to a surviving spouse who does not have interest or experience in managing investments.

And if you have any inkling or concern that you— or a spouse—may one day suffer cognitive decline, an income annuity becomes one of the kindest decisions you can make for yourself, your partner, and your kids.

Yes, your kids. For those of you with children, if you eventually become cognitively impaired, won't it be your kids who step in and help you keep things running? The simplicity of an income annuity will make it easier on all of you.

Look, I know no one wants to think about this. But to not consider the possibility of dementia or Alzheimer's is irresponsible. We can all hope breakthrough treatments are going to emerge in our lifetime. We can all take better care of ourselves to maybe tilt the odds our way or at least forestall our mental decline. We can pray and hope we retain our mental faculties. And yet none of that offers us any guarantee we will be spared.

We don't control the cognitive gods. Yet what is absolutely in our control is thinking through ways to do some advance financial planning that can provide insurance for a later-life "what if": What if I can no longer carefully handle my financial accounts?

An income annuity requires no management once you buy it. There are no portfolios to rebalance. There are no bear markets to worry about. Once the money is handed over to an insurance company, that is money you won't be tempted to use to chase after a hot stock or a deceptively high yield. It is also money that will be out of the reach of an unscrupulous cheat who preys on seniors, especially seniors who may not be as mentally sharp as they once were. Tucking some money away with an insurer provides protection from elder financial abuse.

Income annuities take all of those issues off the table. No matter what happens to you, the monthly payout just keeps getting deposited in your checking account. You don't have to keep up with anything, and no one can interfere. How is that not valuable insurance to consider?

The older you are when you start payments, the more money you will receive. You can wait until you are ready to retire—say, age 70—and buy an immediate annuity. Or, with a deferred annuity, you pay the premium today (or over a few years) with the agreement that payments won't start for another 5 or 10 years, or more.

And here is something to chew on: Academic research and surveys of retirees report that people who have guaranteed income are happier and more secure in retirement. Security is a powerful asset, both financially and emotionally.

That said, I want you to know that if you absolutely, positively won't consider an income annuity because of the loss of control, yet you very much want more guaranteed income, the insurance industry has rolled out income annuities with bells and whistles just for you.

There are now income annuities that basically provide a death benefit of sorts.

An income annuity with a cash benefit will pay you a lifetime benefit, but if you die before your total payouts equal the up-front premium you paid, your beneficiary will continue to get payments until total payments equal what you paid for the income annuity.

Another option is an income annuity with a fixed benefit. You (or a beneficiary) are guaranteed to receive payments for the "fixed" period you choose; it can be 5 years, 10 years, or 20 years.

You can get quotes for income annuities with and without these features. Your monthly payout will be less if you choose one of these options that ensures you "get back" something. A plain-vanilla income annuity will be the best financial choice, but if you can't will yourself to consider that, then you may find it a worthwhile trade-off to buy an annuity that will keep paying even if you die sooner rather than later.

AN ANNUITY TO HELP CALM LONGEVITY FEARS

If your retirement were to last just 15 or so years, you probably would be pretty calm. You likely have plenty of income sources you can draw on for such a relatively short time.

But as I explained earlier in the book, there are some pretty strong odds that you may live into your 90s. Being sure your money will be able to keep supporting you for 25 or 30 years is a tougher proposition.

If your worry is that your money will run out if you have the good fortune of a very long life, a longevity annuity may be worth considering. Longevity annuities are basically deferred income annuities, but their start date is way off in the future. You pay your premium today, but the payments don't start until you are 80 or 85.

Because of the long lag time—during which you could die—the premium on a longevity annuity is much lower than on an annuity that starts payments earlier. For example, in late 2019, a 70-year-old woman who spends $100,000 for a longevity annuity would receive a monthly payout starting at age 85 of around $1,500 a month. Before she turns 91, she will have received her initial investment back, and the payments will continue for the rest of her life.

If you are interested in a longevity annuity, you may want to consider purchasing one with money in a 401(k) or IRA. These are called *Qualified Longevity Annuity Contracts (QLACs)*, and they offer a temporary reprieve from paying RMDs.

The money you use from a traditional 401(k) or IRA to purchase a QLAC is no longer counted as part of the balance on either type of account, which will reduce your RMD. For example, if you have $500,000 in a traditional IRA, your RMD will be calculated as a percentage of that $500,000. But if you used $100,000 to purchase a QLAC, which will begin payments years from now, your balance for calculating your RMD is now $400,000. (Once payouts begin at 80 or 85, you will owe income tax on the payments.)

You are allowed to use 25% of a retirement account balance, up to a maximum of $135,000 (in 2020), to purchase a QLAC.

You can buy income annuities and longevity annuities online through websites that will collect your information and then give you instant quotes from a handful of insurers. Immediateannuities .com (www.immediateannuities.com) and Income Solutions (www.incomesolutions.com) sell annuities to individuals. The Go2Income site (www.go2 income.com) provides instant free estimates of various types of income annuities based on pricing at more than a dozen financially strong insurances companies; it also offers an annuity shopping service for customized quotes. Your discount brokerage might offer an annuity service, and some 401(k)s also offer annuities to participants. If you work with a fee-only financial planner, they will be able to help you consider your options and direct you to the best solution for your needs.

You can use money in an IRA or 401(k) to purchase an immediate annuity, or regular savings from a taxable account.

If you use money currently invested in a traditional 401(k) or IRA, the process essentially works like an IRA rollover: You move the money over to the insurer, who will put the money in a "qualified" account that is essentially an IRA. Then you will pay income tax on the distributions just as you would if money had remained in a traditional 401(k) or IRA.

If you use after-tax savings to purchase an immediate annuity, you will not owe tax on the portion of the payment that is a return of your investment, but any earnings on your annuity that are part of the payment will be taxed.

When you are shopping for an immediate annuity, you should receive (or request) estimates of how your payments will be taxed.

A crucial part of your buying process should be to confirm that the insurance company is in strong financial shape. After all, you are handing this company a lot of money that you expect to collect on for decades, or in the case of a longevity annuity, that you won't even start collecting on for a few decades. When you get quotes, the financial strength rating of the company should be prominently displayed. If not, just do a web search of the name of the insurer and the term "financial strength ratings." There are a few major ratings companies; the ones most widely used are Standard and Poor's, AM Best, and Moody's.

Each service has its own scale that starts with AAA or A and declines to CCC grades or lower. I would not invest with any company that has any form of a grade with even the letter B. Please stick with a company that has a very high rating from at least two of these rating companies:

Standard & Poor's: AAA, AA, or A
AM Best: A++, A+, A, A-
Moody's: Aaa, Aa1, Aa2, Aa3

Keep at least two years of expenses in cash.

Those of you who've been following my advice for years know that I have long said every household needs an emergency fund that can cover up to eight months of living expenses.

I also want you to have a separate bear-market emergency fund in retirement that has at least two years of living expenses in it. If you expect that you will not cover all your living expenses from guaranteed income, then I would recommend keeping three years of expenses in super-safe accounts that you can tap whenever you need to and know the money will be there for you.

Let me be clear: This is in addition to your eight-month emergency fund.

Why such a big bear-market emergency fund? To give you the confidence that you can handle whatever the markets—or life—throws at you. This is money you can live on no matter what happens. And we all know things happen. When all your money is tied up and then something happens and you need to tap that money, that is when you will lose money. For instance, when a bear market hits, rather than pull money from your stock investments when they are lower in value, you can use this money to cover expenses. That in turn can make it emotionally easier to not sell your stocks when they are down.

This fund is also where you get the money to pay for out-of-pocket medical expenses if you suffer an injury or serious illness. It can also make it easier to hire help while you are recuperating.

You should create this bucket of cash from your bond portfolio. For instance, let's say you have $500,000 in investments that is split $250,000 in stocks and $250,000 in bonds. And let's assume your annual living costs are $35,000. I would move at least $70,000 (two years of living costs) of your bond portfolio into savings accounts, certificates of deposit (CDs), or short-term bond funds with a duration of no more than two or three years. In this example you would keep $70,000 super safe and invest the remaining $180,000 in intermediate-term Treasury notes, or in funds or ETFs that own short- or intermediate-term Treasury issues.

CONSIDER SAVING ONLINE

I know many of you do your banking at a bank or credit union that has local branches where you can use an ATM or speak with a teller. That is a fine place to keep your checking account and get easy access to cash at the ATM when you need it. But banks with physical branches—called *brick and mortar*—tend to not pay the best interest rates on savings accounts and CDs.

Keep your checking account right where it is, but I want you to consider moving your savings to an online bank or credit union that pays higher yields. A big reason they can pay higher yields is that they don't have physical branches with rent and overhead. In late 2019, when many traditional banks were paying 0.25% or less on savings accounts, some high-yield accounts had yields of near 2% or so. The interest on CDs also tends to be much higher at online banks and credit unions.

You can link your online account with your checking account, and transfer money with a few mouse clicks.

Savings accounts and CDs you purchase through online bank and credit union accounts are completely safe. They are no different from the same types of accounts at a traditional bank. And they offer the same federal insurance coverage.

It's easy to confirm that an online account will be federally insured. For a bank, scroll to the bottom of the bank's homepage and you will see an "FDIC insured" logo. For a credit union, keep an eye out for a small logo with the acronym NCUA. The National Credit Union Administration is the federal program that provides insurance to credit unions; it works the same as FDIC insurance for banks.

At a bank or credit union, you will have a minimum $250,000 of insurance protection at a single bank for all your insured accounts: checking, savings, and CDs. So you and your spouse could each have $250,000 of coverage in separate accounts. If you also have a joint account, that is eligible for another $250,000 of insurance coverage per person.

Need more than that? Depending on the type of account, you may be eligible for even more coverage at your current bank. Or you can open accounts at another bank and repeat all the coverage limits. But I want to be extra clear here: It must be an entirely different bank, not merely a different branch of the place where you currently bank.

BE CAREFUL: NOT EVERY TYPE OF BANK AND CREDIT UNION ACCOUNT IS FEDERALLY INSURED

Federal insurance protects only certain types of accounts you buy and hold at a bank or credit union.

Accounts that are covered by federal insurance:

- Checking accounts

- Savings accounts

- CDs

- Money market deposit accounts

In the rare event that your bank or credit union runs into financial difficulty, federal insurance will step in and repay you every penny in those accounts, up to the limits discussed above.

But banks also offer (sell) many types of investments that are not covered by this insurance.

Investments you can buy at a bank that will not be backed by federal insurance:

- Stocks and bonds

- Mutual funds and ETFs

- Annuities

- Life insurance

> Honestly, if you want to make any of those investments, a bank or credit union is likely a lousy place to be shopping. Banks and credit unions typically offer investments that charge higher fees than a discount brokerage, or a service that specializes in life insurance or annuities. And now that you know those accounts don't qualify for any federal insurance at a bank or credit union, why bother buying there? Save money and do your investing and insurance buying elsewhere.

A web search of "high yield online savings" will direct you to sites that track the best offers. Or at the Deposit Accounts website (www.depositaccounts .com), you can use its free search tool to look for offers. Be sure to read the fine print on the required minimum balance and whether there are any limits on how many withdrawals you can make in a month. That shouldn't be an issue, as you will still use your regular checking account for paying bills; chances are you likely won't need to make withdrawals from an online savings account more than a few times a year, if that much.

BUILD A CD LADDER

You may also want to consider keeping all or a portion of your safe savings in a certificate of deposit (CD). Online banks and credit unions also offer CDs.

CDs are a savings vehicle that lasts for a set period of time. You can purchase one-, two-, three-, four-, and five-year CDs. The longer the "term," the more interest you will be paid. The interest rate will not change over the duration of the CD. Your interest rate is locked in on the day you purchase. If you think rates are going to go down, a CD can be a better place for your safe money than a savings account, where the rate can fluctuate.

CDs are just as safe as regular savings accounts. When the term ends—often referred to as when the CD *matures*—the money you invested in the CD, your principal, will be returned to you.

There's one catch with CDs. If for some reason you decide you need the money before your CD matures, you can take it out but you will pay an early withdrawal penalty. The penalty varies according to the term.

A one-year CD will typically charge an early withdrawal penalty of three months or so of interest. For a five-year CD, the penalty might be six to eight months interest. Every CD issuer has its own policy. Be sure you know the rules before you invest.

A portfolio of CDs with different maturities can be a smart strategy to increase your overall yield, while reducing the chances you will need to make an early withdrawal. For instance you could invest equal amounts in five different CDs: one-year, two-year, three-year, four-year, and five-year. That way you have some money maturing every year. When the one-year CD matures, invest it in a new five-year. Your two-year CD now has just one more year to go, so it becomes your one-year CD. When it matures, invest that in a five-year CD too. Keep doing this and eventually you will have a portfolio of five-year CDs, with one maturing every year. That will pay you more interest than if you kept all of your money in a one-year CD that you had to reinvest annually.

I think the CD ladder can be a terrific option for some of your cash, but if you are aiming for a two-year cash reserve, I would still keep at least six months of that in a simple savings account where you will not owe any withdrawal penalties.

CONSIDER MONEY MARKET MUTUAL FUNDS

A money market mutual fund at the discount broker-age where you have your IRAs and other investment accounts can be a good option for savings as well. Just keep in mind that money market mutual funds are not federally insured. If you save in a money market mutual fund that owns U.S. Treasuries, I don't think you need to worry about insurance. The fund is full of rock-solid securities. That said, if you feel bet-ter knowing your savings are federally insured, stick with a high-yield online bank savings or CD account.

HATCH AN RMD PLAN

If you have savings in a traditional 401(k) or a tradi-tional IRA, the federal government is going to force you to start taking money out each year starting by the following April 1 once you turn 70½ (if born on or before 6/30/49) or 72 (if you were born after), if you are retired. Still working? You are required to start withdrawals from your IRA and any old 401(k)s from previous jobs, but you can delay RMDs from your current 401(k) until you stop working.

For those of you who have saved some money in Roth 401(k)s (covered in Chapter 3), there is an odd quirk you need to know about. You will be required to take distributions if the money is still in the Roth 401(k) the following April 1 once you turn 70½ (if born on or before 6/30/49) or 72 (if born after). Don't worry: You won't owe tax on the withdrawal. But every year you will need to take the RMD. If you don't need the annual distribution, it is smarter to move the money from a Roth 401(k) to a Roth IRA so you can keep the money growing tax free. Rollovers are explained in Chapter 3, and once the money is in the Roth IRA, you are not obligated to make any withdrawals.

The reason you are forced to take money out of traditional accounts, as I noted earlier, is that the federal government is eager for you to pay income tax on the money. Remember: That's the deal you signed up for when you chose to save in a traditional 401(k) or IRA; you got a tax break on the money you contributed— it was deducted from your taxable income for that year—with the understanding that in retirement you would owe income tax on withdrawals.

Even if you don't have the financial need to touch these accounts, you still must start making annual withdrawals. The federal government sets the floor on what you must take out each year—by now you know this is called your Required Minimum Distribution (RMD). It is a formula that requires you to withdraw a set percentage of your traditional accounts each year. The percentage is based on the balance of your account on December 31 of the prior year.

The calculation adjusts for your age. Someone who is 70 will have an RMD equal to 3.65% of the value of a traditional account. By age 75 the RMD is 4.37% of the value. At age 85 you are required to withdraw at least 6.76% of the value of a traditional retirement account. If your spouse is at least 10 years younger than you and is sole beneficiary of an account, your RMD will be based on a different calculation that will slightly reduce your RMDs.

Learn more. At my website, I have worksheets that will show you what your RMD percentage will be each year. Go to suzeorman .com/retirement.

Because the RMD is based on a percentage of your year-end account value, the dollar value of your RMD will fluctuate along with the performance of your portfolios and the changing required percentage you must withdraw. For example, you are 70½ and because you were born on or before 6/30/49, your required

RMD withdrawal is 3.65%. You have $1 million in your 401(k), so your RMD will be $36,500. Then let's say a bear market hits and your portfolio value falls to $800,000 by the time you are 72. Your RMD percentage will be higher—3.91%—but because your portfolio is smaller, the value of your RMD will be $31,280. The reverse is true in roaring bull markets, of course. If your $1 million portfolio grows to $1,200,000 at 72, your RMD will be nearly $47,000.

Don't worry: You don't need to do the RMD calucation yourself. The company where you have your IRAs and 401(k)s invested will calculate your RMD for you. You can set up an automated system to make the RMD by the year-end deadline (though you can take it out earlier in the year too). I recommend making your RMDs automatic. There is a massive penalty for missing an annual RMD: 50% of what you were supposed to withdraw. Ouch!

Technically, you don't have to take your first RMD until April 1 of the year *after* you turn 70½ (if born on or before 6/30/49) or 72 (if you were born after). My advice is that if you are retired, start the RMDs in the year you turn 70½ or 72. Don't delay to the following April. If you delay you will still be required to take another RMD by year end for your current-year RMD. Having to make two RMDs in one calendar year is going to push your taxable income higher, which might bump you into a higher tax bracket, impact the taxation of your Social Security benefits, and even mess with the premium you will owe on your Medicare Part B coverage.

RMD'S WHEN YOU HAVE
MULTIPLE ACCOUNTS

For those of you thinking it makes sense to add up all your RMDs from different accounts and then just take the money from one account, I couldn't agree with you more. But aggregating and making one withdrawal is not allowed in some instances. Here's what you need to know:

- **IRA RMDs:** You can calculate all the RMDs from your IRAs and then, if you want, take that total sum from just one account. You don't have to make withdrawals from each IRA.

- **403(b) RMDs:** Same treatment as IRAs. If you have multiple 403(b)s, you can take your total RMD for all the accounts out of a single account.

- **401(k) RMDs:** No dice on taking the total RMD from just one account. You must take an RMD from each 401(k) account, every year.

Married? Be very careful. You aren't allowed to add up your household's total RMDs and then pull the money from one (or more) accounts. Retirement accounts are in individual names only. Each of you must take all the RMDs required from your individual accounts, following the guidelines mentioned above.

If all of that just gave you a headache, remember that you can consolidate accounts under one roof with IRA and 401(k) rollovers, which can make it far easier to manage RMDs. (See Chapter 3.)

You Don't Have to Spend All of the RMD (and Probably Shouldn't)

Just because you must make withdrawals from your traditional retirement accounts, that does not mean you can or should spend all of it. After you pay the IRS their tax, what you do with your distribution is entirely up to you. For many of you, it will be wise to consider reinvesting some of your RMDs.

In the next section, I will explain why starting your retirement spending at no more than 3% of your portfolio value is a good target to aim for. You can then plan to increase your withdrawal by the rate of inflation each year.

That means that if all of your retirement money is in traditional accounts, your RMDs will be more than the 3% rule. In that case you can reinvest a portion to keep your actual spending to around 3%.

You can't reinvest an RMD in your IRA or 401(k) when you are retired. You would put the money in a "regular" taxable account. Regular accounts are taxed differently from the money in your traditional 401(k) and IRAs.

In a regular account, interest income will be taxed at your ordinary income tax rate. If you invest in bond index funds or bond ETFs, you will indeed have annual interest income. Even if you reinvest that income in the same fund/ETF, you will still get a tax bill each year. Keep in mind that income from Treasury bonds is typically exempt from state income tax. And municipal bond income is typically tax free on your federal return and may be tax free on your state return as well.

If you own index mutual funds or ETFs, you will typically not owe any other tax until you sell shares, and then only if you sell for a profit. I want to be clear: This is not true of actively managed funds or ETFs you own in a taxable account. Actively managed funds can produce tax bills every year that you are a shareholder if a manager makes portfolio changes that cause the fund to "realize" gains on a sold investment. By law, funds must pass along the majority of those gains. In the next chapter, I will explain why low-cost index mutual funds and ETFs are the best way to build a diversified portfolio. The fact that both types of investments don't typically generate capital gains tax while you own shares is an extra reason to stick with them when you are investing in a regular taxable account.

When you do sell shares in an index mutual fund or ETF, the tax on any profit will likely be a lot lower than you expect. When you sell shares at a profit, that is called a *capital gain*. And for regular accounts, capital gains have their own tax rules.

When you sell an investment you have owned for at least one year, the profit will be taxed as a long-term capital gain.

For most of you, your long-term capital gains rate will be either 0% or 15%.

LONG-TERM CAPITAL GAINS TAX RATES		
	0% long-term capital gains	15% capital gains tax rate
Single	Income $0 - $39,999	$40,000 - $441,450
Married, filing a joint tax return	Income $0 - $79,999	$80,000 - $496,600

For 2020, incomes above $441,450/$496,600 pay a higher capital gains tax rate.

Shares that you own for less than one year and sell for profit are considered short-term gains. Short-term gains are taxed at your income tax rate.

One added benefit of taxable accounts is that you can claim a tax break if you sell shares at a loss. That's not possible with 401(k)s and IRAs.

There are short-term losses and long-term losses. How you apply them depends on a few factors.

If you have a short-term loss (you sell an investment you have owned for less than one year, for less than it cost you to buy the shares) and you also have a short-term gain, you must first use the loss to reduce the size of your taxable gain. The same goes with long-term losses: They must first be applied to reducing any long-term capital gain you had from selling shares in the same calendar year. If you only have a short-term loss and a long-term gain (or vice versa), you are allowed to apply either loss to either gain.

If you don't have gains to offset, or they don't offset all your losses, you can also deduct up to $3,000 of your remaining losses from your income on your current tax return. If the loss is more than $3,000, you can carry over your loss balance into the next tax year and go through the same exercise. There is no limit on how many years you can "carry forward" a loss.

I want to make one thing clear: You can claim losses on taxable investment accounts, but this break is not available if you sell your primary residence at a loss. While the tax law gives you a big tax break if you sell your home at a gain, it provides no relief when you sell a home at a loss.

Given that bond funds and bond ETFs produce a lot of interest income (taxed at your income tax rate, not capital gains), you may want to consider owning those investments inside your 401(k)s and IRAs where you won't owe tax until you make a withdrawal. And focus on using regular taxable accounts for your stock investing, where your taxes will come mostly from gains when you sell, not income.

Some good news for my fellow dividend-stock investors: The best sturdy dividend stocks—and the index funds and ETFs that invest in them—make distributions that typically qualify for the long-term capital gains treatment. This "qualified dividend income" will be taxed at whatever your long-term capital gains rate is. As I mentioned earlier, that's typically going to be 0% or 15% for most of you.

If you choose to work with an advisor, a good one will be laser focused on helping you manage your investment tax bill. If you want (or need) to sell some shares at a gain, an advisor may be able to help you identify shares of another investment that may currently be worth less than what you paid; by selling shares in that investment, you can reduce (and maybe eliminate) the tax due on your capital gain.

Plan to spend no more than 3% of your portfolio in the first year of retirement.

As I said before, you may be familiar with a popular withdrawal strategy that suggests you start by withdrawing 4% of your money from your accounts and then adjust that amount each year by the rate of inflation. For instance, if you have $1 million, you would withdraw no more than $40,000 in your first year. The next year, if inflation was 3%, you would withdraw $41,200 ($40,000 plus 3%). If inflation was 3% the third year, you would withdraw $42,436, etc.

This advice was based on research that found that if you kept 50% of your money in U.S. stocks and 50% in Treasury bonds and you started withdrawals at age 65, there was a near 100% probability that your money would last for at least 30 years, based on historical returns.

I still think this can be a good approach to consider, but given that I always want you to be more than okay, my recommendation for those of you retiring in the next few years is to consider spending just 3% of your portfolio each year. As I have already explained, your RMD will be higher than 3%. What I am suggesting is that after taking your RMD and paying the tax, you reinvest some of your money so that your net withdrawal rate works out to just 3% in the first year of retirement. (You can adjust that for inflation each year.)

My concern is the strong possibility that the returns we may earn on our stocks and bonds will be lower for the next decade or so.

As I write this in late 2019, the stock market is 10 years into a bull market. Stocks have climbed so much in value during this bull market that we should not be surprised if stock returns for the next 10 years will not be as strong. High-quality safe bonds are also likely to produce lower returns in the coming decade given that yields are so low right now.

In a scenario where portfolio returns are lower than the historic norms, a safer strategy would be to spend less of your RMDs in the early years of retirement.

That said, if all your living costs will be covered from guaranteed income—Social Security, pensions, and maybe income annuities—a 4% net withdrawal rate is less risky. Even if returns are lower, there is still a high probability you will be just fine.

Moreover, the estimates of how long your money will last are based on starting withdrawals at age 65. If you wait until age 70 to start, then 3.5% or 4% can make plenty of sense, as your retirement years have been shortened from 30 to 35 years down to 25 to 30 years.

The most important factor is whether you retire in a bull market or a bear market. If you have the misfortune of retiring just as a bear market hits, or you encounter one in the first 5 or so years of retirement, withdrawing as little as possible is going to be a huge help 10, 20, 25 years down the line. A bear market is a punch to your portfolio. Taking money out is another blow that leaves the account even more depleted. By scaling back withdrawals as much as possible, you can give your money more time to recover. (Congress waived RMDs in 2009 for just this reason: After the big bear-market losses, it didn't want to force retirees to pull money out of their accounts.)

In the next section, I explain a strategy that can help your portfolio survive bear markets.

STAY FLEXIBLE

A key component of your retirement income plan is to stay flexible as your situation shifts and modify your plan when needed.

This is no different from how you have navigated your entire life. By the time you are 50, 60, or 70, you have spent decades making plans and then adjusting those plans as life dictates. That's such a valuable muscle you have exercised often. I want you to keep using it in retirement.

For example, if you decide to start with the 3% withdrawal strategy with an annual inflation adjustment, that is not some written-in-stone strategy. If you suspend the inflation adjustment in years when your portfolios are down, you increase the life span of your portfolio. In very bad down markets, reducing your withdrawals by 10% or so from the prior year is also going to help you navigate through a rough stretch. (For example, if you were withdrawing 3.3%, you would reduce your withdrawal to 3%.)

Maybe a vacation or two gets delayed or you trim your monthly entertainment spending. Reducing or suspending cash gifts to your kids and grandkids isn't selfish; it's how you protect your kids from one day having to step in and provide financial support. These likely aren't forever cuts, but are important ways to counteract the risks that rise when portfolio values are down. When they have recovered, you can raise your spending rate.

I also want to make sure you remain flexible if you have the good fortune of retiring into a bull market, which keeps your portfolio growing even as you are making withdrawals.

If that is the wonderful predicament you land in, I hope you will allow yourself to spend more later on, if that is something that would make you happy. Maybe it is spending on you; maybe it is spending on loved ones. Maybe it is sharing more with the causes that are meaningful to you.

I am not giving you license to spend more indiscriminately. I am suggesting that if you are the beneficiary of good fortune in the markets, and if want to take advantage of that, you should give yourself permission to spend on things that matter to you. Do a thorough review of your situation—or work with an advisor who can run the numbers—and you may find you have the flexibility to increase your spending 10 or 15 or 20 years into retirement and still retain ample savings that will see you through safely and dependably.

YOUR ULTIMATE RETIREMENT CHECKLIST

❏ Estimate your monthly income in retirement.

❏ Aim to cover essential living costs from guaranteed income sources (Social Security, pensions, income annuities).

❏ Be open to income annuities (the "good" annuities) as a way to create more guaranteed income.

❏ Keep at least two years of living expenses in cash if you won't cover everything from guaranteed income.

❏ Be ready to take your annual RMDs once you turn 70½ if born on or before 6/30/49, or 72 if you were born after that date.

❏ Consider reinvesting some of your RMDs early in retirement.

CHAPTER 7

HOW AND WHERE TO INVEST

Okay, now, deep breath. That last chapter was a lot, I know. But once you have had a chance to process it all, I hope it will have made you feel more in control of your money. Creating a strategy that can cover all (or most) of your monthly living costs from guaranteed income sources such as Social Security is the surest way I know to reduce financial stress. And now you know how to hatch a plan that will cover most if not all of your needs from guaranteed income.

At the same time, many of you have investment accounts that you will tap in retirement. The money you withdraw from 401(k)s, IRAs, and taxable accounts is not guaranteed; this is money you have invested, and thus its value will rise and fall based on what is happening in the markets.

In this chapter we will focus on how to invest your retirement accounts. I know this can often be very stressful for many of you. You want to make sure the money in your 401(k)s, IRAs, and regular investment accounts will continue to support you for decades.

I understand where your anxiety is coming from. But as your kids (or grandkids) would say, "You got this." By the end of this chapter, I promise, you will understand what to do. I also want to be clear that I am 100% supportive of you hiring a financial advisor if you don't want to be totally responsible for the investing decisions. But first I want you to understand the strategies at work in investing. What you learn in this chapter will help you vet a financial advisor; if an advisor's advice dovetails with what we cover here, then you can be confident you've found someone good.

However, before we settle into discussing the moves to make, I want to be absolutely clear about one decision you should never, ever, be tempted to make.

NO FREE LUNCH

You and your investment accounts are going to be very popular as you near retirement. It's as if you have a big sign on your back that says, "I am retired and not sure how to invest my 401(k) and IRA." You will be amazed at the letters, e-mails, and maybe even cold calls you will get from financial advisors eager to manage that money for you . . . for a fee, of course.

I want you to steer clear of any advisor inviting you to a free (!) retirement investing seminar. And no, don't think you can just show up for the free lunch that is often a part of the seminar. It may seem like just a harmless sandwich to you, but I promise you, it is all too easy to get lulled into buying whatever the advisor is selling.

These seminars are often run by advisors who want to sell you expensive investment strategies and products that will earn the advisor a big fat commission or fee. And these people are so polished and friendly that it is easy to believe whatever they are pushing is a great deal.

Look, if you want investing help, that's a great thing to know about yourself. But you are to do the research to find an advisor you can trust (lots more on this in the next chapter). I seriously doubt a great advisor needs to run a free-lunch seminar. My advice is to steer clear.

IT'S NOT REALLY ANYTHING NEW

The main thing to know about investing in retirement is that how you invest that money really doesn't change much from what you have been doing for decades in workplace retirement plans and IRAs.

Your 401(k) likely offered you mutual funds (low-cost index funds, I hope) to invest in. You owned a mix of stock and bond funds. Even if you decide to roll over your 401(k) to an IRA, you will do exactly the same. As I explained in Chapter 5, discount brokerages such as Fidelity, Schwab, TD Ameritrade, and Vanguard will help you set up and execute a 401(k) rollover, moving the money from an old 401(k) to an IRA account. Every discount brokerage offers terrific low-cost (and even, in the case of Fidelity, no cost) index funds and exchange-traded funds (ETFs) that work just like the funds you had in your 401(k).

In retirement you are going to keep investing in much the same way. You will want to have a diversified portfolio. You will want to keep your costs low. And you will want to land on a mix of stocks and bonds that will strike the right balance for you in providing some long-term growth—you have to plan for inflation over a long retirement—and the safety that becomes so very important as the years go by.

THE MOVES TO MAKE WHEN INVESTING YOUR RETIREMENT ACCOUNTS

- Plan on living to at least 95; 100 is even safer.

- Make inflation fighting part of your plan.

- Set your retirement asset allocation strategy.

- Use low- or no-cost index mutual funds or exchange-traded funds.

- Choose the right stocks to own in retirement.

- Choose the sturdiest bonds to own in retirement.

Plan on living to at least 95; 100 is even safer.

I sort of hope you are going to be annoyed with me in a second. I am going to repeat advice I have already laid out a few times in this book. It bears repeating because it is the central decision that will help you build a durable retirement income plan that can support you for decades.

That's right—I am going to mention longevity one more time. If you don't need any more convincing why someone in good health today should base their retirement plan on living to at least 95, and 100 if they want to be extra safe, then I have done my job!

But I worry that many of you don't really think about that older you. Research has shown we find it hard to connect to our future older self. We are focused on the here and now. That often leads to caring only about whether you can pay the bills this year and next year. But you're not exactly focused on how you will pay the bills 20 or 30 years from now.

So let's tackle this one more time: Unless you have a medical condition today that you have been advised will shorten your life, I want you to set your investing strategy on the assumption that you will have a long and great retirement that lasts 25 or 30 years.

SUZE'S STORY

When my dad died, my mom was 66 years old. My dad had left her some money, but not much. My mother wasn't worried about the money. Her parents and grandparents had died in their 60s, so she felt that she didn't have many years left.

My mother didn't die in her 60s. She lived to be 97.

By her early 80s, her savings were gone and all she had left was Social Security. I am so grateful that I was in a position to step in and help. I was already managing her money, and when it ran out, I never told her I was covering her bills. I think deep down she knew, but at the same time she wanted to think she was supporting herself with money Dad had managed to save.

I think about her whenever I am talking about retirement planning. When she was in her 60s, she couldn't imagine living until 97. If you are like my mother and can't imagine living well into your 90s, please push yourself to at least set your investing strategy as if you will. It's good for you and for your loved ones. Even if you have family that can step in and help, I know that deep down you would prefer to remain independent. Even if, like my mom, you live to be 97.

Make inflation fighting part of your plan.

Okay, okay, no more longevity talks. But now we need to make sure your investing plan will work for a very long time. When your investing-time horizon stretches out 30 years, you must take into account that your living costs decades from now will be more than your costs today.

Think about the car you bought 30 years ago. Or the house you bought 25 years ago. Or the cost of college 40 years ago. You are aware that all those things cost a lot more today. A whole lot more. The inflation you have experienced throughout your adult life is not going to magically disappear in retirement.

If your plan is to stay in a home you own, your property tax, insurance, and maintenance costs will be higher in the future. If you rent, you will see those costs passed along to you over the years. Travel costs rise. If you need some help along the way, the cost of that care, be it assisted living or an aide who visits you at home, will be higher in the future than it is today.

While it is true that inflation is low these days, that doesn't mean you can afford to ignore it. Even at a low rate of 2%, inflation will have a big impact on your cost of living. If inflation were to run at 2% a year for the next 20 years, you will need nearly $1,650 to cover $1,000 of expenses today.

And I think it is dangerous to assume that just because inflation is low today, it will always be low.

As a planning exercise, I want you to look at how a 3% average annual rate of inflation will impact your expenses. Mind you, 3% is higher than the current rate, but it is still less than the longer-term norm.

At a 3% annualized rate of inflation, here's what you will need to spend in future years to pay for $1,000 of expenses today:

WHAT $1,000 TODAY WILL COST IN . . .	
5 years:	$1,160
10 years:	$1,340
25 years:	$2,090
30 years:	$2,430

Rounded to the nearest dollar.

So that leads us to our first investing challenge: How should you invest your retirement money today to keep pace with inflation?

The answer: stocks.

Yes, stocks.

Over decades stocks have, on average, delivered returns that are above the rate of inflation. Cash in a credit union or bank has typically not kept pace with inflation. Intermediate-term bonds have done a bit better than cash, but they aren't designed to provide strong inflation-beating gains either.

Now, of course, there is a problem with stocks. They go through periods when they fall in value, and that tends to scare people off. But that doesn't mean it is safer to pull all your money out of stocks in retirement. If you keep everything in cash, or high-quality

U.S. Treasury bonds, what's your plan for being able to afford the higher cost of living that inflation will bring you in 10, 20, 30 years?

The bottom line is that for most of you, stocks are likely to be a necessary part of your investing plan.

STOCKS IN MODERATION

I am not suggesting you keep all your money in stocks. No way! My message is that you should keep *some* money in stocks. If you are in your 50s and 60s today, depending on your situation, you should already have a significant portion of your portfolio—maybe half—invested in bonds. But the other half of your investable assets most likely are in stocks.

DON'T RUN FROM BEAR MARKETS

We discussed this in the previous chapter, but it bears (!) repeating: Please don't avoid stocks because you think they are too dangerous. What is more dangerous is just having your money sit in accounts earning 1% or so and spending down your principal too quickly to meet your expenses.

If you have a solid allocation strategy, you will own some stocks and a lot of bonds. The bonds are what make it emotionally and financially possible for you to keep owning stocks. Even if a bear market hits, you will have a big chunk of your money in bonds. As I explain later in this chapter,

Treasury bonds are the best bonds for retirees. And in a bear market for stocks, Treasury bonds tend to rise in value. So when a bear hits, if you are already retired and taking withdrawals from your accounts, you will take it from your bonds and leave the stocks untouched.

BEAR WITH IT

One of the best things about being an older investor is that you know bear markets don't last forever, and patience is your biggest asset. On average, the loss in a bear market is around 35%, the slide lasts about a year, and then it takes on average another two years for stocks to get back to where they were before the fall. You will have plenty of money in bonds and dividend-paying stocks to cover your income needs for those three years. Even if you need to give your stock portfolio six years to recover—that's about how long it took for the bear market that began in 2007 and ran through the financial crisis to play out and for stocks to recover—you will have more than enough invested in bonds to carry you through.

And as I covered in the last chapter, if the majority of your living expenses can be covered from guaranteed income—Social Security, a pension, an income annuity you purchase—you are in an even better position to calmly ride out a bear market.

Set your retirement asset allocation strategy.

How you divide your investing pie between stocks and bonds is a very personal decision. I have some recommendations, but I want to stress that there is no single best allocation strategy that is right for everyone.

Everyone's goal is to land on a plan that brings them confidence and peace of mind. You, and only you, know what feels right.

My goal is to give you some clear-eyed insights on what to consider.

For instance, there is a rule of thumb that can help you start to think through how much of your investments you want to keep invested in stocks.

Subtract your current age from 110. That is how much you may want to consider keeping in stocks.

For example, if you are 65 you would subtract 65 from 110, which is 45.

So you would have 45% of your portfolio in stocks.

If you are 70, having 35% in stocks can make sense.

The idea behind this straightforward calculation is that you will have plenty of bonds to provide stability for you, while also keeping some of your money invested in stocks to produce inflation-beating gains. As the years go on, you can adjust; at 80 or 85, you might want to consider ratcheting down your stock holdings. Or maybe the markets will have been so good that you now have all the money you could ever need, but you want to keep investing in stocks with an eye toward growing the money for your heirs.

That is just one guideline. You need to think through what your needs are. If you have all your living expenses covered by guaranteed income, you might consider investing more in stocks. After all, you aren't relying on the stocks to help you pay current bills.

But I also want you to seriously think through what I call your emotion quotient: How will you feel if in retirement there is a bear market like the one that began in late 2007? I am not suggesting the next one will be as ferocious, but for this exercise, it is a good gut check. You probably weren't retired then, but I bet you remember what it felt like. Were you able to stick to your investment plan, or were you sick with worry?

Realize that in retirement, your emotions can play an even bigger role. When you are no longer being paid a salary, the tendency is to be extra focused on what is happening to your investments. If you panic, that can lead to bad decisions.

If you talk yourself into a stock allocation that makes you nervous, you will likely be tempted to sell stocks after they have lost value; you just can't deal with the upset. And that is the wrong time to sell.

In 2008 so many people sold stocks because they were scared. They felt good about their decision because it brought immediate relief. But those same people didn't have the nerve to get back into stocks. They sat on the sidelines, maybe earning 1% on that money during a bull market that began in 2009 and is still running as I write this in late 2019. Even if they eventually got back in three, four, or five years later, they already had missed out on some big gains.

It makes no sense to set a strategy that will cause you anxiety and may lead you to make rash, emotional decisions.

That said, I am not giving you a free pass to steer clear of stocks. The far better move is to reduce the amount you have in stocks. If the rule of thumb we discussed would suggest having 45% in stocks, maybe you lower that to 40%. If the target is 55%, maybe you reduce that to 50%. Small reductions. Not totally bailing out.

If you simply can't see yourself owning a significant amount of stocks, that is an important stand-in-your-truth decision that I respect. But if you make the decision to not own stocks, or to own a very small amount, you also need to stand in the truth of what that decision may mean for your financial security.

If you have less money invested in stocks, you may not have enough money earning inflation-beating gains over the long term, which means you may not be able to afford the higher costs of living when you are 80, 85, 90. You have traded one risk (stock market volatility) for a new risk (your money doesn't keep up with inflation).

That will require taking other steps to be able to afford the higher cost of living decades from now. One way to plan for those higher costs is to look for ways to spend less now so you have more in your retirement pot for those later years. As I explained in

Chapter 3, living below your means today will make it possible to still be able to pay tomorrow's inflated living costs.

Another strategy is to not spend your entire RMD proceeds. As we discussed, you must take RMDs from traditional retirement accounts by April 1 once you turn 70½ if born on or before 6/30/49, or 72 if you were born after. (The one exception is if you are still working; in that case you don't have to take an RMD from the 401(k) at your current job.) But there is no rule that you have to *spend* your RMD withdrawals. As I explained in Chapter 6, you can reinvest all or a portion of your RMD. I think that becomes a major consideration if you have decided to sharply reduce your investment in stocks. The money you reinvest essentially becomes your new fund to help you afford inflation years from now.

I also want you to be extra careful about how you invest if your guaranteed income won't be enough to cover your living expenses. Some of you will be tempted to own more stocks, to make more money. That is the worst thing you can do. Even if they are dividend stocks.

You can't afford to gamble like that when you are relying on your portfolio to buy the groceries, cover your housing costs, and pay for utilities. In a bear market, your total portfolio might take a 30% or 40% hit. If that happens and you need to make withdrawals from the bruised portfolio to cover living costs, you are digging yourself a deeper hole that can put your security at risk. When a bear market hits, your goal should be to not touch the stock portion of your portfolio. You want to give it time to nurse its way back. Once you take money out of a portfolio that is already down, it is gone forever.

Use low- or no-cost index mutual funds or exchange-traded funds.

After you decide on the right mix of stocks and bonds, successful investing requires nailing just three key moves:

1. Own a lot of different stocks and bonds.

Diversification is the technical name for this. Owning low-cost mutual funds and ETFs is the easiest and most efficient way to be a diversified investor. If you want to invest in individual stocks, I want you to be careful to remain diversified. My advice is that no single stock should ever account for more than 4% of the money for the stock side of your portfolio. For example, if you were to own only individual stocks, my recommendation is to have a portfolio of at least 25 stocks, with no stock representing more than 4%. It is too dangerous to have bigger investments in a single stock; you can't take the risk of having a big bet that goes bad, causing your portfolio to tumble. I myself own more than 25 stocks.

2. Don't try to beat the market.

There are two major camps of investing: indexing and active.

Indexers invest in a basket of stocks or bonds that track a benchmark, such as the Standard & Poor's 500 stock index. Indexing is often referred to as "passive" investing, because there is no manager behind the scenes making calls on what to buy or sell.

Active investors are trying to beat the performance of an index.

It makes perfect sense to think that active investing is the way to go. Who doesn't want to beat the market? But active managers have a lousy record. The vast majority of investment pros don't produce returns that are better than their target index. And even when an active manager pulls off that tough feat for a year, or two, or three, the odds are slim that over the long term an actively managed fund will consistently do better than a "boring" index fund.

It's not that investment pros aren't smart. Some do a great job. But all funds charge investors an annual fee, called the *expense ratio*. Actively managed funds charge higher fees than most index funds, and once those fees are deducted from an active fund's gross return, the net that goes into your account is typically less than it would be if you invested in a low-cost index fund or ETF.

That brings us to the final, crucial, rule of investing:

3. Use no- or low-cost index mutual funds or exchange-traded funds (ETFs).

Both index mutual funds and ETFs are fantastic ways to own a diversified portfolio. When you invest in a mutual fund or ETF, you become an instant owner of dozens—and often thousands—of individual stocks or bonds.

Your job is to make sure that the mutual funds or ETFs you own are no or low cost. There are terrific no- or low-cost index mutual funds, and terrific low-cost ETFs. You can use either, or both. All that matters is sticking with low-cost options.

A quick review of both options:

MUTUAL FUNDS

You are no doubt familiar with mutual funds; they are the backbone of most 401(k)s, and you likely own a few in an IRA. (Many 401(k)s offer a collective investment trust [CIT]; it's a version of a mutual fund made especially for the 401(k) that typically has very low fees.)

Mutual funds are a fine way to invest your retirement portfolio if you follow three rules:

- **Focus on no-load mutual funds.** When you and I started investing, many mutual funds were sold by brokers who charged a sales commission, known as a *load*. The good news is that load funds have become very unpopular. There is no reason you should ever pay a sales commission to own shares of a mutual fund. Period. No-load mutual funds are the way to go. The major discount brokerages, such as Fidelity, Schwab, TD Ameritrade, and Vanguard, offer plenty of no-load mutual funds.

- **Choose index mutual funds.** There are two types of mutual funds: index funds and actively managed funds. This bears repeating: Actively managed funds don't consistently beat index funds, in large part because they charge higher fees. You are better off investing in index funds.

- **Use index mutual funds with low expense ratios.** Mutual funds—and ETFs, for that matter—charge an annual fee, called the *expense ratio.* Some actively managed mutual funds charge an annual expense ratio of more than 1%, while many index mutual funds charge an expense ratio of less than 0.10%. (See the box on page 212 for why expense ratios are a very big deal.)

All the major discount brokerages offer no-load index mutual funds that have no or low expense ratios. There is no reason to pay more than 0.10% a year to own a broad U.S. stock market index fund. Some charge 0.03% a year. Fidelity has four ZERO index mutual funds that do not charge any expense ratio at all.

EXCHANGE-TRADED FUNDS

ETFs are very similar to index mutual funds. They are a diversified portfolio of dozens of securities. The main difference has to do with how often their price is set.

A mutual fund's price is set just once a day, after the market closes at 4 PM ET. If you place an order to sell shares of a mutual fund at, say, 11:15 in the morning, the price your shares will be sold at will be based on the closing price of all the stocks (or bonds) in that fund at the end of the trading day; in this example that's nearly five hours later.

An ETF works like an individual stock. During the day, when the stock market is open, the price of an ETF will move along with the value of the securities it holds. If you place an order to sell ETF shares at 11:15 in the morning, the transaction will be priced at whatever the share value was at 11:15 when the order was processed.

ETFs are popular among professional traders, where instant market pricing is crucial. But it really shouldn't be a front-of-mind issue for you. If you have a long-term investment strategy—and that is what your retirement portfolio is all about—you don't need the instant pricing of an ETF. When you are investing money for decades, waiting a few hours for the market to close and your sale (or purchase) price to be set isn't going to make or break your retirement.

I want to be clear; ETFs are a fine way to invest your retirement money, but not so much because of the fact that you can buy and sell during the trading day and get a market price. For a long-term investor like you, that's not a key consideration. The value of ETFs is that the vast majority track indexes; very few ETFs are actively managed. And index ETFs can have very low expense ratios.

That said, there can be a flat fee when you buy or sell ETF shares. Because ETFs trade like a stock, you may be charged a sales commission. The commission to buy or sell ETF shares can be $20 to $25 per trade. However, all the major discount brokerages—Fidelity, Schwab, TD Ameritrade, Vanguard—offer some ETFs that you can buy and sell without paying a commission. It makes sense to stick with no-fee ETFs.

Note: If you have accounts at a full-service brokerage that charges a commission on ETF trades (and mutual fund trades for that matter), I want you to be sure that you are getting value for keeping your money there. As I explain in Chapter 8, I think working with a financial advisor who relies on commissions isn't the best approach.

THE BIG PAYOFF FROM PAYING ATTENTION TO EXPENSE RATIOS

The annual fee that mutual funds and ETFs charge, called the *expense ratio*, can seem like small potatoes. The highest expense ratios typically aren't more than 1%. It doesn't sound like much, right?

Oh, but it is. Investing in an index mutual fund or ETF that charges a very low expense ratio—say, below 0.10%—can give you thousands of dollars more to spend (or save) throughout your retirement.

The expense ratio is not a line-item cost that you see in your statements. It is a cost that is deducted behind the scenes from a fund or ETF's gross return. For example, let's say a fund has a gross return of 6% and it charges a 1% expense ratio. The net return that will be credited to your account is 5%.

Let's say that instead of investing in a fund that charges a 1% expense ratio, you use a fund that charges a 0.10% expense ratio. Assuming the same 6% gross return, your account will be credited 5.9%.

If you invest $100,000 in a fund that earns a 5% net return (after deducting a 1% expense ratio), your account will be worth $105,000 after the first year. If instead you earned a 5.9% return (after deducting the 0.10% expense ratio), your account will be worth $105,900. You kept $900 more simply because you smartly chose a low-cost fund. That's just for year one. Over 20 years the compounding growth of that money adds up: Your $100,000 will be worth nearly $315,000 if you earned a 5.9% annualized gain, compared to around $265,000 if you earned a 5% annualized return.

Now do you see why I think low expense ratios are a very big deal? Adding tens of thousands of dollars of income—or inheritance—without taking on more risk is an opportunity you should never pass up. Low-cost index mutual funds and ETFs are the way to go.

Choose the right stocks to own in retirement.

Okay, so we've established that you want to own some stocks, and either no-load index mutual funds or no-commission ETFs are the smart way to build a diversified portfolio.

That leaves one huge question: What types of stock funds or ETFs should you own?

I have long believed in a straightforward approach that divides your stock portfolio into two pieces:

- 85% invested in a broad "total" market U.S. index fund or ETF.

- 15% in an international index fund or ETF.

A broad U.S. index fund or ETF is a one-stop way to own thousands of stocks that come in all sizes. You will own the big stocks, called large caps (Amazon, Microsoft, Berkshire Hathaway) as well as mid-cap and small-cap companies.

A stock's market capitalization is the value of its stock multiplied by the number of shares. A stock with a market cap of at least $10 billion is typically considered large cap. Many large caps actually have market caps in the hundreds of billions. As I write this in late 2019, Microsoft has a market cap of more than $1 trillion. Small caps are typically companies with a market cap below $1 billion. Mid caps are between $1 billion and $10 billion.

I know many of you use an S&P 500 index mutual fund or ETF as the foundation of your stock portfolio. The stocks in that index are mostly large-cap stocks. There is nothing wrong with that! But about 20% of the value of the U.S. stock market comes from companies that are mid cap and small cap. When you invest in a total stock market fund or ETF, you are getting the large companies plus the smaller ones too. I think that is worth considering.

If you want to move money from an S&P 500 index fund to a total stock market index fund, there will be no tax bill if the exchange is inside a 401(k) or IRA account. If you own the shares in a regular taxable account, talk to your tax pro before making any move. When you move money from one fund to another fund in a regular account, you are selling shares to buy shares. Any sale in a regular taxable account that results in a capital gain will trigger a tax bill. It can still make sense to make the change, but your tax pro will be able to advise you on how to minimize the tax hit.

It's easy to pinpoint total market funds, as they typically have "total stock market" in their name. For instance, there is the Vanguard Total Stock Market Index Fund, the Fidelity Total Market Index Fund, and the Schwab Total Stock Market Index Fund. Vanguard and Schwab also have ETFs that track the total stock market. Another low-cost ETF that tracks the U.S. market is the iShares Core S&P Total U.S. Stock Market ETF.

Okay, now let's talk about international stocks. I am sure you realize that there are many publicly traded companies outside of the U.S. About half of the global market cap is from companies based outside of the U.S. I totally get the comfort level that comes from investing with a bit of a home bias, but at a minimum I think you should have 15% of your stock portfolio invested in non-U.S. stocks.

A broadly diversified international index fund or ETF will own stocks from developed countries (e.g.,

Japan, Germany, England, Australia) as well as emerging economies (e.g., China, India).

The Fidelity ZERO International Index Fund doesn't charge an expense ratio. The Vanguard Total International Stock Index Fund charges 0.11%, and the ETF version charges 0.09%. The iShares Core MSCI Total International Stock ETF also charges a 0.09 expense ratio.

With two funds, the stock portion of your investment strategy is set. Can you add more? Sure. But I want you to know that if simple is appealing, you will be in great shape if you invest the bulk of your stock portfolio in one broadly diversified U.S. index fund and add a side dish of an international index stock fund.

DIVIDEND INVESTING: YES, IN MODERATION

Dividend investing has long been a staple of retirement investing strategies. A dividend is a periodic cash payout a company makes to shareholders. It can be monthly, quarterly, or annually. Not all companies issue dividends; typically companies with significant profits decide to share some of that with shareholders by giving them a dividend.

The value of that payout divided by a stock's share price is called the *dividend yield*. For example, a stock that has a share price of $50 and makes a $1 annual dividend payout has a dividend yield of 2%. As I write this in late 2019, the S&P 500 stock index has a dividend yield of about 1.8%.

There are index mutual funds and ETFs that focus on dividend-paying stocks, and they tend to have higher dividend yields, about 2.5% or so in late 2019. Some funds that focus on high-dividend stocks pay an even bigger yield.

I think dividend-paying stocks can be appealing for retirees, but only as a complement to a total market fund. It can be dangerous to think that dividend stocks are all you need to own in retirement and you can "live off" the income.

For starters, no stock's dividend is permanent. If the company hits hard times, the dividend can be cut. That happened to many banks during the financial crisis.

And it's important to be aware that a high-dividend yield can be a signal of a company going through a tough period. For example, let's say three years ago a stock paid a $1 dividend and the share price was $50. That's a 2% yield. The company then raised the dividend to $1.10, but the share price is now $25. The dividend yield is now 4.4%. That may look enticing if you want to buy a dividend stock. But you need to ask yourself: Why has the stock price fallen so much? If there is a big problem, chances are the dividend yield could be reduced in the future, and the stock price will keep falling.

Moreover, If you load up on dividend stocks, you will be ignoring some of the most dynamic growth stocks. Over the past 10 years, Amazon, Netflix, Facebook, and Google were some of the most profitable large-cap stocks. None paid a dividend.

If you find dividend stocks appealing, my advice is to make them a small part of your U.S.

stock holdings. For example, instead of having 85% in a U.S. broad market index mutual fund or ETF, you could have 65% in the broad market index fund, and 20% in a dividend fund or ETF. The 15% invested in international stocks wouldn't change.

The one dividend move I will not support is taking money out of your bond holdings to buy dividend-paying stocks. This is a seriously bad move. I am very aware that many dividend-paying stocks yield more than high-quality bonds these days. (More on bonds below.) But the reason to own bonds in retirement is because they are the lifesaver in stormy stock markets. When stocks are in a bear market, Treasury bonds often post gains. If instead you are invested in dividend-paying stocks, you are going to take a bath in a down market. Sure, the 2% or 3% dividend payout may continue. But the share price of the dividend fund or ETF will behave like a stock fund . . . because that's what it is!

I want to be clear: I love dividend stocks. But not as a substitute for bonds. In the bear market that ended in early 2009, the SPDR S&P Dividend ETF—a terrific way to invest in dividend payers— lost 52%, and that included adding in the value of the dividend payouts. Meanwhile, the Vanguard Intermediate Term Treasury Index Fund gained more than 15%. Case closed. If you want to invest in dividend stocks, carve out room from the stock side of your portfolio. Dividend stocks never were and never will be a substitute for bonds.

Choose the sturdiest bonds to own in retirement.

The bond side of your investment portfolio is all about safety. The goal is to own bonds that will stand tallest when stocks are falling. This becomes doubly important in retirement when you will be taking money from your accounts.

If you will be making withdrawals from your investment portfolio, you want to be careful to not touch your stocks during a bear market; you want to let that part of your portfolio recover before you resume taking money from it.

When stocks are down, high-quality bonds will hold their value, and may even rise a bit. If you have 40%, 50%, or more invested in bonds, you will be able to take distributions from this part of your investment portfolio for years without having to touch your stocks.

TREASURY BONDS DELIVER THE SMOOTHEST RIDE IN RETIREMENT

U.S. Treasury bonds are the best option for a retirement portfolio. They are hands down the safest type of bonds. Investors, including foreign governments, own U.S. Treasury bonds because of their rock-solid reputation. Whenever you hear the global stock markets are spooked and there is a "flight to safety," that means investors are flocking into U.S. Treasury bonds.

I want you to be aware that you likely have less than half of your portfolio invested in U.S. Treasuries right now. I am making that educated guess because I know most of you own bonds through mutual funds offered in 401(k)s.

The most popular type of bond mutual fund is called a *core bond fund*. It tracks the Bloomberg Barclays U.S. Aggregate Bond Index. This index is built to mirror the mix of the entire market of high-quality taxable U.S. bonds. In late 2019 about 40% of the index was invested in U.S. Treasuries; the rest was invested in other types of high-quality bonds, including investment-grade corporate bonds.

There is nothing wrong with owning a mutual fund or ETF that tracks this index. But it is not the best option in retirement. If your focus is on owning bonds that will be the most resilient during an economic recession or bear market—and I think that should be the primary focus in retirement—you will want to own only Treasuries.

Looking back to the scary markets during the worst of the financial crisis will give you a vivid picture of why Treasuries are the best option in my opinion. From late August 2008 through late October—less than two months—the S&P 500 stock index fell nearly 35%. The Bloomberg Barclays U.S. Aggregate Bond Index lost more than 5%. The Vanguard Intermediate-Term Treasury Index Fund broke even during that extremely stressful period.

The reason the Aggregate lost more than Treasuries is because the Aggregate owns corporate bonds and other high-quality types of bonds. A corporate bond is a loan a company takes out. In the midst of the financial crisis, when corporate stocks were plummeting and the economy was in trouble, corporate bonds became riskier too. It's not that there was concern about corporate bonds issued by financially strong companies going bankrupt. But in a period of extreme stress, jittery investors are going to feel better in Treasuries or cash than in the bond of a private company.

That 2008 example is indeed the most extreme during our lifetime. Let's hope it stays that way. And again, I want to be clear that there is nothing wrong with sticking with a core bond fund that tracks the Aggregate. It's just that Treasuries will deliver a smoother ride.

Indeed, during the full length of the 2007 to 2009 bear market for stocks, the Aggregate bond index did a fine job. During a stretch when the S&P 500 lost 55%, the Aggregate bond index gained 7.2%. Treasuries did even better; the Vanguard Intermediate-Term Treasury Index Fund gained 16.7%.

If you own Treasury bonds in a regular investment account (not a retirement account), you will owe federal tax on the interest you earn. But Treasury bond interest is not taxed at the state or local level. For those of you in states with high income tax rates, that can make Treasuries even more of a deal than corporate bonds.

FIGHT THE TEMPTATION TO CHASE AFTER HIGHER-YIELDING BONDS

As I write this in late 2019, Treasury bonds that mature in 10 or fewer years have a yield below 2%. Ever since the financial crisis, Treasuries have not paid interest above 3.5%. I understand how frustrating that can be when you are retired and want to earn as much safe income as possible.

Are there higher-yielding bonds? Of course. You could stick with a core bond fund that mirrors the performance of the Bloomberg Barclays U.S. Aggregate Bond Index and earn a higher yield than a Treasury-only portfolio. If you are okay with the fact that in rough markets, your Aggregate fund will not hold up as well as a Treasury fund, that is a reasonable trade-off to consider.

As I just explained, the Aggregate index owns high-quality bonds; sometimes you may hear these bonds referred to as *investment grade*. This means that the entity that issued the bond is considered to be in good shape financially and should be able to pay interest on time and repay the principal value of the bond when it matures.

What I never want you to do is invest your retirement bond money in any fund or ETF with the name *high yield* in it. These are funds that invest most of their money in bonds from issuers who are not exactly on the firmest of financial ground. You want to know another name for high-yield bonds? Junk bonds.

Junk bonds are the worst idea for your retirement bond portfolio. I know their yields look tempting. While intermediate-term Treasury funds have a yield below 2% as I write this, junk bonds have yields of more than 5.5%.

Now let's talk about the trade-off you make if you chase after the higher yields of junk bonds. Junk bonds are issued by corporations that can fall into deep trouble when a recession hits, by companies with iffy financials, or in industries that are struggling. That's why they pay a higher yield! It's the only way to attract investors.

The problem occurs when the economy is having a hard time. Junk bonds will suffer losses that are more in line with what you would expect from stocks. During the very rough market in September and October 2008, when an intermediate-term Treasury fund broke even, a high-yield bond fund lost 26%. Not 2.6%, but 26%.

If you want higher-interest payouts, whether from junk bonds or other income-oriented funds, the money should come from the stock side of your investment portfolio. Because in a down market, junk bonds are going to perform a lot like stocks.

FOCUS ON INTERMEDIATE-TERM BONDS

Bonds are loans. The issuer, be it a government or a corporation, agrees to pay back the face value of the bond on a specific date. That date is referred to as a bond's maturity. Bonds have maturities that range from 1 year to 30 years or more.

The issuer also agrees to make periodic interest payments—monthly, quarterly, or twice a year is typical—to investors until the bond matures.

Short-term bonds mature in less than 5 years. Intermediate-term bonds mature in 5 to 10 years. Long-term bonds mature in 10-plus years.

The longer a bond's maturity, the higher the interest payment—called *yield*—the issuer will typically pay. That is, longer-term bonds typically have higher yields than intermediate-term bonds, and intermediate-term bonds typically have higher yields than short-term bonds.

However, I don't want you to own long-term bonds.

When general interest rates rise in the economy, long-term bonds suffer bigger price declines than shorter-term bonds. Conversely, when interest rates fall, longer-term bond prices rally. As I write this in late 2019, interest rates are very low. I doubt you need me to point out that yields on bonds have been extremely low since the financial crisis more than a decade ago. We may be in for an even longer period of low rates, but given where we are today, the risk to watch for is that rates could eventually rise.

That's a reason to avoid long-term bonds.

If you stick with me for a quick explanation of one bond statistic, you will see what I am talking about. Every bond mutual fund or ETF publishes on its website the portfolio's duration. It is expressed as years. A short-term bond fund might have a duration of 1.8 years, or 2.7 years, for example. A core bond fund that tracks the Bloomberg Barclays U.S.

Aggregate Bond Index has an intermediate duration of about 5.5 years. Long-term bond funds can have durations of 10 years, 15 years, or more.

A fund's duration is a guide for what will happen to the price of the fund's bonds when interest rates change. For a fund with a 5-year duration, a 1 percentage point rise in interest rates will cause prices in that fund to fall 5%. If the duration is 2.7 years, the price decline will be around 2.7%. If the duration is 12.8 years, the prices of bonds in that fund will, in aggregate, fall about 12.8%.

Yes, it is absolutely true that when rates fall, longer-duration funds and ETFs will have the biggest price gains. But I don't think investing with an eye toward rates falling from their current low levels makes sense. The risk we need to focus on is what might happen to your bond investments if interest rates were to rise.

Duration only tells us what you might expect to happen to the price of the fund and ETF. You are also collecting the interest those bonds are paying out. Your return is the combination of changes in price plus the yield you are collecting. The combined value of the price change plus the yield is what is known as a fund's *total return*. This is the value reported on your statements.

Let's say a fund with a 5-year duration has a 2.5% yield. Over the course of a year, interest rates rise 1 percentage point. That would send the price down 5%, but you also collected interest that rose from 2.5% to 3.5% during the year, so your total return was a loss of less than 2.5%. If after that rise, rates stabilize, so too will prices. And you will soon be back in positive territory, as you are now collecting a higher yield: 3.5% in this example.

The main takeaway from all this is that given where the U.S. economy is—and where global economies are—focusing on intermediate-term bond funds and ETFs is a smart balance between risk and reward. You will earn more interest than a shorter-term bond fund, without the big price swings of longer-term bond funds.

That said, I have no problem if you want to put some of your bond portfolio in shorter-term funds. That will be an even smoother ride in rough markets, but again, you need to understand the trade-off: You will earn less interest than if you focus on intermediate-term bonds with durations of around five years.

AN INFLATION TIP

In addition to plain-vanilla Treasury bonds, I also recommend you consider owning another type of Treasury bond called *TIPS*. That stands for Treasury Inflation-Protected Security. The protection is that when inflation rises, the value of the bond is adjusted higher.

To be clear, if prices go down (deflation), the value of a TIPS would also fall. That would be an extremely rare event. For your long-term retirement planning purposes, I am more concerned that your portfolio be invested with an eye toward making sure you can keep up with the likelier scenario that living costs will increase over time.

You can buy TIPS directly at TreasuryDirect.gov, but you will be in charge of handling the dividends and reinvesting when the bonds mature. There are a handful of low-cost mutual funds and ETFs that simplify investing in TIPS. Vanguard Inflation-Protected Securities owns TIPS with an average duration of around seven years. Vanguard Short-Term Inflation-Protected Securities Index Fund has a duration of less than three years. Both can be bought as a mutual or an ETF. The Schwab U.S. TIPS ETF has a duration of around seven years.

WHAT ABOUT MUNICIPAL BONDS?

Municipal bonds, also referred to as *tax-exempt* or *tax-free* bonds, can be a solid complement to Treasury bonds. The interest you earn on a municipal bond is typically not taxable on your federal tax return, and if the bond is issued by your state, you will also be able to avoid any state income tax on the interest.

Municipal bonds have become more popular since the big tax reform package became effective in 2018. The current tax law severely limits itemized deductions. For many higher-income households in states with high income tax rates and high property tax bills, the loss of itemized deductions has caused their tax bills to rise. That makes municipal bonds attractive; tax-free income sure looks appealing when your tax bill has gone up.

That said, I recommend that you not invest 100% of your retirement bond portfolio in municipal bonds. Keeping some money in Treasuries will help you navigate any possible hiccups that can impact municipal bonds:

IN A RECESSION, MUNICIPAL BOND JITTERS CAN INCREASE.

A municipal bond is issued by a government—state or local—or an agency that provides a public service, such as water or transportation services. The bond issuer pays the interest from revenue it takes in. That can be state and local tax collections, property taxes, or fees we all pay for services. In a recession, the money municipalities take in can fall.

Municipal bond issuers defaulting on interest payments is extremely rare. But during an economic downturn, the municipal bond market will not offer as smooth a ride as Treasuries. To give you an idea, let's return to the fall of 2008 when the financial crisis was at level-10 intensity. An index of municipal bonds lost 5%; a fund invested in intermediate-term Treasuries broke even.

STAYING "IN-STATE" CAN BE RISKY.

Interest on municipal bonds is generally 100% tax free on your federal return, regardless of what state the bond was issued in. On your state income tax return, only the interest earned from bonds issued within your state are eligible for tax-free treatment. There are many single-state municipal bond funds that make it easy to focus on only in-state bonds.

A common strategy for residents in states with high income taxes is to own only "in-state" municipal bonds. This can be risky. Many states lack a diversified portfolio of municipal bonds that are being used for different projects and have varying revenue sources. California and New York have broadly diversified municipal bond markets, but I would advise caution if you are considering a single-state fund within a different state—especially if you live in a state that is grappling with big budget challenges. Again, I am not suggesting that bankruptcy is the risk, but the less financially strong an issuer is, the bumpier the ride will be in bad economic times.

Sticking with a national municipal bond fund or ETF can be the smarter move. As its name suggests, a national portfolio will own funds from many states. That's valuable diversification. The interest you receive will be tax free on your federal return, and the portion of the interest that came from bonds in your state may be deductible on your state tax return. (At tax time the fund will tell you what percent of income came from in-state bonds.)

A mutual fund or ETF is the best option; unless you have a million dollars or more to invest just in municipal bonds, the fees you will pay to buy the bonds are going to be too high, and you likely couldn't build a diversified portfolio of issues.

The iShares National Muni Bond ETF and the Vanguard Tax-Exempt Bond ETF both track an index of high-quality municipal bonds, have durations between five and six years, and charge annual expense ratios below 0.10%.

Municipal bonds are one market where active management can make sense. There is no central marketplace where municipal bonds are traded, such as the New York Stock Exchange and NAS-DAQ for stocks. That makes pricing less uniform in the municipal bond market. An active manager can take advantage of that. And an active manager has the leeway to pick and choose among different types of municipal bonds. For example, a bond that is tied to a steady source of revenue can be less volatile during a recession than a bond that is tied to general tax collections. In muni bond lingo, "essential revenue" bonds are more reliable than "general obligation" bonds. Active managers have the freedom, if they want, to own more revenue bonds and fewer general obligation bonds than an index fund.

The Vanguard Intermediate-Term Tax-Exempt Fund is an actively managed mutual fund that focuses on high-quality issues. Its duration is around five years, and it charges a low 0.17% expense ratio. The Fidelity Intermediate Municipal Income Fund is another active option; it charges 0.37%.

YOU CAN BUY TREASURIES DIRECTLY FROM THE U.S. GOVERNMENT

All U.S. Treasury bonds have a AAA credit rating. That means you don't really need to worry about building a diversified portfolio of Treasuries. I still think mutual funds and ETFs are a great way to own Treasuries (more on this below), but I also want you to know that you can buy individual Treasury bonds at the government's TreasuryDirect.gov website (www.treasury direct.gov).

The technical name for Treasuries that mature within 2 to 10 years is *Treasury notes*. Treasuries with a shorter maturity are called *Treasury bills*. Treasuries that mature in more than 10 years are called *bonds*. You'll need to know what type of Treasury you want, as the website divides instructions for each type across different pages.

Some discount brokerages, including Fidelity, Schwab, and Vanguard, will help you buy Treasuries through the government auction, without charging a commission.

Owning a portfolio of individual Treasuries can be a fine way to go, but please candidly consider your interest in staying on top of things. You will need to decide what to do when bonds mature and what to do with your interest payments. You are effectively taking on the job of bond fund manager—your own personal bond fund. Even if that appeals today, I ask you to also consider what will happen as you grow older; will you still be able to manage your investments? Managing a portfolio of individual Treasuries could become a challenge. And if you are married and only one of you has interest in running an account at TreasuryDirect, I think it is best to stick with bond funds or ETFs to simplify things.

CONSIDER NO- OR LOW-COST MUTUAL FUNDS OR ETFS

For ease of use, a Treasury mutual fund or ETF is a smart option. The no-load Fidelity Intermediate Treasury Bond Index Fund charges a rock-bottom 0.03% annual expense ratio. The Vanguard Intermediate-Term Treasury Index Fund has an average duration of around five years and charges an annual expense ratio of 0.07%. An ETF version of this fund also charges a 0.07% expense ratio. Vanguard also has a short-term government fund and ETF.

The Schwab Intermediate-Term U.S. Treasury ETF charges a 0.06% expense ratio, as does the Schwab Short-Term U.S. Treasury ETF.

Those are just examples; my advice is to search for the lowest-cost Treasury options at whatever brokerage you have your money with. Just remember: With a mutual fund you never should pay any sales commission, called a *load*. And check whether your brokerage offers Treasury ETFs that you can buy and sell without paying a sales commission.

DON'T FEEL COMPELLED TO DIY

I am confident you have all it takes to build a portfolio of two stock funds/ETFs and one or two bond funds/ETFs. But there is no reason you should feel pressured to do this on your own.

I know I have just given you a lot to digest. I imagine you may have already marked some pages to return to. That's exactly what I expect! It takes time to absorb information and decide what is right for you.

And I want to circle back to what I consider the most important part of retirement planning: that you feel confident in your choices and thus don't have to think about the money stuff (at least not too often).

Please do not feel rushed to make choices. Never make a move when you aren't sure whether it is right or not. It is always better to do nothing than to do something you don't understand. Nor do I ever want you to feel embarrassed that you don't understand something. You should be proud that you are taking the time to learn.

If you find that you just can't get comfortable with the responsibility of overseeing your investments, that's more than okay. If hiring a financial advisor gives you confidence, that is the right move for you! It can also make tremendous sense if you are concerned about cognitive decline later on. All I ask is that when you work with a financial advisor, you only approve strategies that you understand. What happens to your money impacts you. Even when you hire someone, you need to stay engaged. The good advisors will be eager to talk things through with you; they know how important it is for you to be comfortable and confident in how your money will be invested.

In the next chapter, I discuss how to find a reputable financial pro. Many advisors provide financial planning advice and will also manage your investments for you. Or you can hire an advisor to recommend an allocation strategy and specific funds, and then you can follow through on your own.

There is also another option if your sole focus is getting some guidance on asset allocation decisions. Robo-advisors such as Betterment and Wealthfront charge low fees to manage your account, and they invest your money in no- or low-cost ETFs. The "robo" refers to the fact that the base level of these services does not provide a fully personalized portfolio; the allocation advice is from a series of set strategies that take different approaches to risk and reward.

Vanguard and Schwab also now offer low-cost advisory services that will help you find the right allocation strategy.

United Income is a tech-driven advisory firm that specializes in helping retirees devise strategies for converting their retirement accounts into a sustainable paycheck throughout retirement; there are varying levels of personalized service that have different fees. But the advisory fee is less than the typical 1% fee regular advisors charge.

Congratulations on getting this far! Again, I know there is a lot of information to digest in this chapter. Take. Your. Time. You can dip back in and review the information as many times as it takes for you to form a sense of what will work best for you. Patience, my friends.

Considering buying real estate to rent out for retirement income? That can be a fine strategy, but assess the risks and expenses first. My website has info and advice to help you make the right decision: suzeorman.com/retirement.

YOUR ULTIMATE RETIREMENT CHECKLIST

❑ Plan for your living costs to rise—a lot—over a 20- to 30-year retirement.

❑ Don't bail on stocks: They offer the best chance of inflation-beating gains.

❑ Aim for a mix of stocks and bonds that you can stick with through good and bad markets.

❑ Create a diversified portfolio with low-cost index mutual funds and exchange-traded funds.

❑ Use a total stock market fund or ETF as the core of your stock investments.

❑ Use dividend stocks in moderation.

❑ Focus on high-quality bonds: Treasuries, TIPS, and (in moderation) municipal bonds.

CHAPTER 8

FINDING THE RIGHT FINANCIAL ADVISOR

I have always said that the best financial advisor you will ever meet is staring at you in the mirror.

I still believe that.

The decisions you make for how to spend your money, invest your money, save your money, and share your money impact you more than anyone else. And you know you best: what matters most to you, what risks you can live with, what will cause you great anxiety.

At the same time, I am all for working with an advisor at this stage of your life if having help will give you confidence and reduce—or even wipe out—financial stress.

Managing your money, focusing on your money, and handling your money should not be a centerpiece of retirement. Anything but! My hope is that in the pages of this book, you will find the guidance you need to help you put a plan into motion today that then makes it possible to focus more on enjoying your retirement without too much worry about your money.

However, if getting that strategy in place seems a bit daunting, or you've got more questions than answers, that's a reason to seek out professional advice.

As you have learned thus far in the book, there are so many choices—and so many moving pieces—that go into building a secure financial plan once you retire. And in many instances, one decision can change the math for a different issue.

Moreover, you will likely need to exercise a completely new set of financial muscles. For decades your savings muscles have been getting a workout. I sincerely hope that while you were working, you did your very best to contribute to retirement accounts; along the way you learned how build a portfolio with stocks and bonds to create the right mix of reward and risk that worked for you. But I have a feeling that many of you never really understood why you made the investment choices you did. If that's the case, then I hope you will reread Chapters 6 and 7 and refer back to them as needed as you are called upon to make investing decisions.

And now you need to flex an entirely new set of muscles: spending the money you have been saving, but doing so at a pace that will make your money last 25 to 30 years.

Are you overwhelmed by the thought of that? I get it—it's a lot to contemplate and juggle on your own.

Even if you are confident that you've got a solid plan, you might feel even better, and be able to truly relax a bit more, if you had someone look it over and give you a second opinion or simply watch over it all for you.

SUZE'S STORY

It may surprise you to learn that I myself have a financial advisor. I like knowing that when I am away, someone is watching my investments. I like having someone to discuss ideas with and make sure I have not missed anything. But my advisor knows not to make a move without my okay. I am totally in control of my money even with an advisor. That is what I want for you as well if you choose to use an advisor.

KT and I met 20 years ago, when we both were already financially secure. When we committed to each other, we made the decision to share our household expenses but keep our investing portfolios separate. I am in sole control of my money, and KT handles her own. That said, we are constantly using each other as a sounding board. In fact our approaches to saving and investing are very much in sync.

I realize our approaches may be a bit different from yours, and I am aware many couples have a hard time getting on the same page about all the financial decisions that come with retirement. I think an advisor can be a terrific resource to help you build a cohesive approach. A knowledgeable, reputable, and impartial advisor can also help you avoid the bickering and tension that can arise when the two of you are faced with making these consequential decisions.

Even if you are capable of handling everything on your own, it's more than okay to decide that you don't want to. You're allowed to move over to the passenger's seat and have someone else drive.

Here's another scenario: If you know that your spouse will never be comfortable handling the finances, it can make sense to build in some support in the event you pass first. My strong recommendation is that when a spouse or life partner dies, it is so very smart for the survivor to not have to make any major financial decisions for at least a year, as they navigate the emotional drain. If having an advisor on board will make it more practical for the surviving spouse to not feel in a rush to make any consequential decisions, that is something to consider.

A financial advisor can also be a wonderful insurance policy you buy today that can protect you if cognitive decline becomes an issue.

The good news is that you can find a financial advisor who fits your specific needs. There are pros who will work with you on a single project and charge an hourly or project fee. If you are looking for a full-service relationship where someone oversees your investments, that's an option too. Just want a little bit of portfolio hand-holding? There are low-cost "robo-advisory" services that might be a great fit.

The challenge is that you need to put in some work to find the right financial advisor for you.

NOT ALL FINANCIAL ADVISORS WILL HAVE YOUR BACK

What you need to know is that anyone can call themselves a financial advisor. Many who use this title are nothing more than salespeople focused on getting you to buy financial products that earn them money.

To state the obvious, salespeople masquerading as financial advisors are to be avoided. That it is legal for them to operate despite the glaring potential for conflict of interest is irrelevant. In this chapter I am going to explain how to find qualified professionals dedicated to helping you meet your financial goals. An advisor who has achieved a high level of financial education and acts in a client's best interests is the gold standard. You should settle for nothing less. I will also share with you the specific ways to vet a financial advisor.

THE MOVES TO MAKE TO FIND THE RIGHT FINANCIAL ADVISOR

- Determine what you want help with.

- Focus on the right type of financial advisor.

- Create a short list of candidates.

- Run a background check.

- The interview: the key questions you need to ask.

- The interview: the questions a great advisor should ask you.

Determine what you want help with.

The best advisor for you depends on the advice you are looking for.

If you want help building your retirement income strategy and running the numbers on a few variables—downsizing the home, waiting until age 70 to claim Social Security—you will want to look for qualified pros who work on an hourly or project basis.

If you are looking for ongoing help, an hourly-fee arrangement can still make sense. In addition to hiring the advisor to help you set up a strategy that you execute, you might agree that you will schedule an annual review, and leave the door open to adding hours for consultations throughout the year.

If you want help running the numbers of various scenarios and building your retirement income strategy, and also want to have your advisor take the lead on managing your investment accounts, you will be looking for a financial advisor who will work on an "assets under management" model. This means they will charge you an annual fee that is a percentage of the investment accounts they are running for you. (Later in this chapter, I will explain how to set up a system for your advisor to manage your money, but with you retaining important control.)

Many advisors who use this model have a minimum account balance for clients; it may be $250,000, $500,000, or more. The annual fee is often around 1%, but there is variation in this rate. For higher account balances, advisors may reduce the charge.

Please note: If the advisor recommends your portfolio be invested in mutual funds and exchange-traded funds, the annual fees for those vehicles are added to your cost. As I explained in Chapter 7, low-cost index mutual funds and ETFs have very low or no fees. When interviewing an advisor who will manage your money, you will want to find out the average annual fees you will pay for your investment choices. More on this soon.

Paying an advisory fee of 1% is not nothing. But it can be a worthwhile price if that advisor executes your strategy well. What your portfolio earns is not the only factor. A good advisor rebalances your portfolio, looks for ways to minimize the tax impact of investing decisions, and perhaps most important, helps you stay committed to your strategy.

The biggest risk to your retirement strategy is how you will react to stressful financial situations. Emotions can be extra powerful when you are retired and aren't earning an income. When stocks are falling, your fear rises and your instinct might be to sell stocks to avoid the pain of the losses. As we discussed earlier, that is a costly mistake you want to avoid. But that emotional reaction isn't you being dumb or irrational; you are being human. It is hard to stay committed to anything when you are feeling vulnerable and threatened.

This is where a financial advisor can earn every penny of their fee. A good advisor will have already spent time with you explaining how your strategy is built to withstand market declines. Then, in the heat of those declines, a good advisor will reach out to you—not wait for you to call, concerned or panicked—and remind you of those conversations, and help you stay focused on your long-term goals.

Your advisor will also be focused on smart bear-market moves and rebalancing your portfolio to make sure you remain on target with your allocation strategy. He or she will also look for opportunities to take advantage of tax-loss strategies; when you sell shares in a taxable account for less than you paid, you will get a tax break on your loss. Harvesting losses and reinvesting the money is a central job a good advisor should perform for you.

Moreover, knowing you have someone to turn to for advice—whenever you need it—can be absolutely priceless if it brings you peace of mind.

HOW TO PAY FOR HELP

There are two ways financial advisors are paid:

Set fee. This can be an hourly fee, a project fee, or an ongoing annual fee that is a percentage of the assets they manage for you.

Commission. A commission is a fee that a salesperson earns when you buy something they recommend, and often when you sell the same investment or product.

The best choice: Fee-only! When it comes to getting unbiased, unconflicted advice that is truly in your best interest, an advisor who only charges set fees, not commissions, is the way to go. You always want to be looking for advisors who state they are fee-only.

Please read that carefully. *Fee-only.* Some advisors will tell you they are fee-based. Fee-based is not the same as fee-only. Fee-based is not good enough. A fee-based advisor might sometimes charge a set fee, and sometimes earn commissions based on what you buy and sell.

I do not recommend working with an advisor who at any time is dependent on selling something to you for their living. That's an inherent conflict of interest that you would need to constantly be on guard for.

Choose a financial advisor who is fee-only.

Focus on the right type of financial advisor.

Broadly speaking, there are two types of financial advisors: financial planners and investment advisors. The lines between the two often blur.

Financial planners are looking at your entire financial picture. A financial planner can create a total plan for you that includes strategies for managing your debts, setting sustainable spending/budgets, and making sure you have the proper level of insurance to keep you safe and protected. A financial planner can help you sort through all sorts of questions: Can you afford to help your adult kids financially? What level of support can you provide your elderly parents without putting your own financial security at risk?

On top of all that, a financial planner can also provide investment advice. Depending on your arrangement, you can get the strategy from the planner and make all the investment moves yourself, or your planner can wear a second hat as an *investment advisor*, who manages your accounts for you.

Some financial advisors are focused solely on investment advice, not broader financial planning. If an advisor is not providing additional financial planning services and is overseeing investment portfolios of mutual funds and ETFs, you should be paying a lot less than a 1% annual fee.

There is also a technological hybrid I want you to know about. Earlier I mentioned "robo-advisors": These are web-based firms that provide a lower level of assistance than a full-service advisor. But that may be all you need.

The cost can be a fraction of a what you pay for full-service advisor because the service relies heavily on technology, not the human touch.

With a robo-advisor, the portfolio advice you receive is generated by a computer algorithm that inputs all the details you share about your age, goals, and appetite for risk. It is automated advice fine-tuned to your personal information. Your money will be invested in low-cost index mutual funds or ETFs. The service will rebalance your portfolio, and some services provide automatic tax-loss harvesting for regular accounts. You can roll over money from retirement accounts into an IRA at the robo-advisory with no tax bill on the transfer. The services will also provide automated RMDs or other withdrawals based on your needs.

Some robo-advisors also offer varying levels of access to a human financial advisor. Betterment and Wealthfront are two robo-advisors with low minimums. Vanguard Personal Advisor Services requires a minimum balance of $50,000. Schwab Intelligent Portfolios has an investment minimum of $5,000. Both offer additional services—including access to financial planning advisors—with higher balances. United Income is a robo-advisor that specializes in retirement issues including the timing of retirement, investment management, and Social Security claiming strategies. Ellevest is a robo-advisor that finetunes its algorithms for female clients to take into account that women typically have different lifetime salary patterns and longer life expectancies.

Create a short list of candidates.

Once you have a sense of the level of help you are looking for, it's time to start looking for that help.

Asking family, friends, and colleagues for references works great when you need a plumber, electrician, or knee specialist. But it's less helpful when it comes to finding someone to help with your money. For starters, someone whose opinion you trust may have a completely different financial situation than you do or a completely different goal in mind. That they like their advisor is great for them, but don't assume that person is going to be the best fit for you. By all means, get references from people you know, but please then follow all my advice on vetting candidates.

You can also use free online search tools to find advisors in your area. That said, if you are comfortable working with someone who is not local—you can have phone and video conference calls—you might want to expand your search outside of your area.

Some places to start your search:

- **Let's Make a Plan** has a web search tool of certified financial planners (CFPs). I am a CFP, so I know how much hard work—including a rigorous exam—it takes to achieve that designation, and the high ethical standards CFPs abide by. Letsmakeaplan.org: www.letsmakeaplan .org/choose-a-cfp-professional/find-a-cfp-professional.

- **The National Association of Personal Financial Advisors (NAPFA)** is limited to fee-only advisors. NAPFA members never earn any money from the investments you buy or sell. Rather than commissions, which can create a serious potential conflict of interest, a NAPFA member is paid a one-time flat fee, an hourly fee, or an ongoing fee that is tied to the money the advisor manages for you. Many NAPFA members will also be CFPs. NAPFA Find an Advisor: www.napfa.org/find-an-advisor.

- **Garrett Planning Network** is a national organization of CFPs (or people working on their CFP certification) who vow to always work in your best interests. GPN members offer financial planning on an hourly, fee-only basis. If you're looking for help with specific questions or crunching the numbers prior to retirement, a GPN member can be a good resource. You can also maintain an ongoing relationship, and some GPN members provide investment advice. GarrettPlanningNetwork.com.

- **WiserAdvisor** and **Wealthramp** are referral services that connect you to potential advisors they think will be a good fit for your needs. The service is free to you. Advisors pay a fee for leads on potential new clients. WiserAdvisor.com, Wealthramp.com.

Run a background check.

I don't care if your three closest friends or the uncle you trust with every fiber of your being recommends someone to you. You must, must, must do your own careful vetting of anyone you are thinking of hiring.

You can learn plenty online.

Check credentials.

All those acronyms after an advisor's name are not to be taken at face value. Some of them sound impressive but are merely marketing gimmicks, not a sign that someone has invested time in becoming knowledgeable about a topic or has passed any sort of screening or exam.

The Paladin Research & Registry website has a free Check a Credential tool where you can plug in an acronym and learn about the quality of that credential; each credential is rated on a scale of one to five stars (www.paladinregistry.com/research/credentials -financial-certifications).

FINRA, the financial service industry's self -regulatory arm, has a free database of professional designations that will give you a sense of the work involved in achieving that designation and what organization is behind it (www.finra.org/investors /professional-designations).

Check for disciplinary and criminal issues.

FINRA also has a free service, BrokerCheck, that will give you background information on financial advisors who work for what are known as *broker-dealers* (brokercheck.finra.org). Not all advisors are affiliated with a broker-dealer. That's more than okay! In that case, their disciplinary record is tracked by the Securities and Exchange Commission. But BrokerCheck makes it easy to check out everyone: If you type in someone's name on the BrokerCheck site and the information you are looking for is at the SEC site, you will be given a direct link to the SEC site.

If you are researching someone who says they are a CFP, you can verify that they are still an active member at the CFP website, Letsmakeaplan.org (www.letsmakeaplan.org/choose-a-cfp-professional

/find-a-cfp-professional). This CFP site also lists disciplinary action, but in the summer of 2019, an investigation by *The Wall Street Journal* found the CFP's system was not thorough, and omitted thousands of disciplinary and criminal infractions that were listed for the same person on the BrokerCheck website. The Association of CFPs is working on improving this feature, but the safe move is to rely on BrokerCheck for vetting bad behavior.

I also recommend you spend some time doing some basic web searches. Type in the name of a person and a series of different keywords, such as "complaint," "lawsuit," "disciplinary action." You can do the same for the name of the person's firm.

And while you're at it, a little bit of sleuthing on Facebook, Twitter, or even Instagram might give you some insights into the personality of the person you are researching. If you have a LinkedIn account, you might also take a look at their profile, connections, and endorsements. Whether someone is into cat videos isn't important, but you may find posts that give you pause, or posts that make you think this is someone you can relate to. It's another piece of information to consider.

If you turn up anything iffy, I would just move on to the next person on your list of candidates. Or if you really think the person could otherwise be a good fit, then you owe it to yourself to ask them directly about the issue that is giving you pause when you interview them.

THE SINGLE MOST IMPORTANT QUALIFICATION: AN ADVISOR MUST BE A FIDUCIARY

I don't think I need to convince you that you want to work with someone who always, always, always puts your best interest first, yet the sad fact is that many people who call themselves financial advisors do not adhere to this standard.

And Washington has absolutely dropped the ball on protecting you. A few years ago, a federal regulation was proposed that would require anyone who provides retirement planning advice to act in the client's best interest above all else. This is known as the *fiduciary standard.* What this means in layman's terms is this:

"If the choice is between advice that is best for you and advice that makes me more money, I will always choose what is best for you." That is what a fiduciary does; they put your needs first.

The financial service industry battled hard to keep this regulation from taking effect. Think about that: The industry that wants you to entrust your money—your future—to them won't promise to do what is best for you. I'm shaking my head as I write this.

Where things stand now is that Wall Street has won. A watered-down version of the regulation, which falls short of requiring an advisor giving retirement advice to serve as a fiduciary, is scheduled to go into effect in June 2020. Merely disclosing any potential conflicts of interest— commissions they will earn, favoring their firm's products over less expensive options—will be all the protection consumers get. Of course, that leaves it up to you to read the disclosure that will explain the conflict of interest. I do not expect the wording to be clear. And once you know about the conflict of interest, what are you going to do? Hire a different advisor?

My advice is to hire the right person the first time.

You can protect yourself with two simple questions for every advisor candidate:

1. Will you always act as a fiduciary? Emphasis on always.

2. Will our client agreement include a written statement signed by you that you will always act as a fiduciary?

The answer to both must be yes. And that yes should come fast, and without hesitation. No trying to explain things, no word salad meant to confuse you. There is nothing to explain. You are entrusting someone with your financial security, and by extension, the security of your loved ones. In return, you should expect this person will operate without any potential conflicts of interest, and be eager to put in writing that you come first.

The Interview: The Key Questions You Need to Ask

Be sure to get an answer on the fiduciary issue before you schedule a full interview so that you don't waste your time. Typically, advisors who are fiduciaries love to advertise that fact on their websites. Then just follow up with an e-mail or call asking whether the advisor will provide a signed document spelling out their commitment.

When you do schedule a conversation with a candidate, I recommend you have a prepared list of questions you want to ask. It is also very important to listen to what questions you will be asked. That can give you valuable insight. (See the next section for a discussion of these.)

If you will be working with someone nearby, I recommend you swing by the office at some point. I would think twice about working with someone whose office is a chaotic mess.

Questions you should ask:

- **Are you a fiduciary? And will you provide a signed document stating you are a fiduciary?** Just to double-check.

- **How long have you been in business?** At a minimum, I want you to work with someone who had clients during the 2007 to 2009 financial meltdown. Experience in trying times is very important. Ask whether at some point you can speak with a current client who was also a client during that stressful time.

- **Am I a typical client?** Does the advisor spend much time focused on the issues that you are looking for help with? If an advisor doesn't have many clients in or near retirement, that should be a yellow light. If you are interviewing an investment advisor with the intent that they will manage your money, find out whether your portfolio size is typical. If an advisor's typical clients have

$5 million and your account is $500,000, that might be an issue. What level of service will you get? If there are five phone calls to return and yours is the smallest account, you might be waiting for a call back. Or you may be directed to work with someone else at the firm. That's not necessarily a problem, but you need to make sure you have confidence in the team.

- **How will I pay you?** Ideally you won't even need to ask about this; it is something an advisor should volunteer. Transparency is a sign of respect and honesty.

  Fee-only is the only right answer. That can be hourly, project based, or an annual percentage of the assets the advisor will manage on your behalf. Also ask what that fee includes. If the advisor will also be preparing your taxes, is that a separate fee, or is that service included? If you are paying a set fee for a one-time big financial plan, how will it work if you need to revise the plan in a year, or two, or three, as life evolves?

- **If you manage my money, what firm will my accounts be with?** In technical terms, your money should be kept with a *third-party custodian*. This is an important safeguard. You never want to send your money directly to the advisor, or a subsidiary of the advisor.

The custodian should be a well-known financial firm. Fidelity, Pershing, Schwab, and TD Ameritrade are popular "custodians."

You also want to confirm that you will have online access to your accounts and that statements will be provided directly from the custodian. If the advisor also delivers personalized statements, that's great too. But it does not replace the need for a third-party statement.

- **If you manage my assets, what would be your general approach?** As you learned in Chapter 7, I am a big believer in low-cost index mutual funds and ETFs being the foundation of a portfolio. Is that the approach the advisor uses? What is the average combined expense ratio for a portfolio that might be similar to what is appropriate for you?

   If an advisor starts crowing about how they beat the market, I would be alarmed. As I explained in Chapter 7, very few money managers have a record of consistently delivering returns that are better than the market average. Besides, what you want to hear is the advisor's approach to creating a portfolio that balances the opportunity for inflation-beating gains with the very important retirement need of managing the level of risk in your portfolio.

Ask how clients fared in the 2007 to 2009 bear market. That's a fair and important question, and the answer includes the advisor's body language and how they frame the response. Every client's experience may be different, but ask about people your age back then: Did they lose more than 30%? Remember: The S&P 500 was down more than 50%. A portfolio that was evenly divided in large U.S. stocks and high-quality bonds—a good barometer for a retirement portfolio—fell less than 25%.

- **If you manage my money, will I have final say on all decisions?** You can give an advisor discretion over your accounts, meaning that investments can be bought or sold without first notifying you or asking your permission. Or you can arrange that all changes first be run by you. I think that is the way to go for at least the first few years. You don't want any surprises, and it's an opportunity to learn more about your advisor's investing strategy in real time.

  At a minimum you want to make sure that your account at the custodian is set up to send you e-mail notifications of all activity on your account.

- **Will I work with you or with other members of your team?** If you are most interested in financial planning advice, and the advisor you are interviewing handles the investing, then you want to interview the person(s) who will be working on your planning issues.

- **When do you expect to retire?** This is only important if you are considering a long-term relationship where the advisor manages your assets. It's natural to gravitate toward people of a similar age, but if you are interviewing someone who is 60, you sure need to hear about the succession plan. Because your hope is that you will outlive the advisor's working days. The ideal situation is that there is already someone, or a few candidates, in line.

  I would think twice about working with a one-person office who is of a similar age. Only because it means you don't have any sense of who might step in, or whether you will be referred to a different advisor in the event that your advisor stops working.

- **Can you provide three client references?** All three should be long-term clients who can talk about how the advisor managed accounts—and nerves—during the 2007 to 2009 bear stock markets.

  Advisors are obviously only going to steer you toward happy clients, but having a frank conversation can still be helpful. Think of what matters most to you and ask questions that might help you get a feel for how well the advisor might deliver.

- **What are your thoughts about my pension? Do you recommend taking a lump sum or the annuity?** For those of you with a pension, this will be a very telling question. An advisor who unequivocally tells you a lump sum is the smart move, before studying your situation, is up to no good. It is rare that the lump sum offered is a better deal. But an advisor may be eager to have those assets to manage so that they can collect their annual fee of 1% or so.

  If an advisor suggests you take the lump sum and invest in an income annuity, it's time to end the interview. Your pension payout is basically an annuity that your employer has created for you. That pension payout is typically going to be a better deal than what you will be paid if you take your pension as a lump sum and then turn around and buy yourself an individual income annuity. Any advisor who suggests you do that is not someone I want you to work with.

  And if the advisor recommends another type of annuity—variable, indexed, etc.—I don't think you are working with a fee-only advisor. Those products are sold by insurance agents masquerading as advisors.

Selling you those insurance products will generate the "advisor" a big commission, and you will have costly ongoing fees. Next!

The Interview: The Questions a Great Advisor Should Ask You

You can judge the quality of an advisor by the types of questions you are asked. Here is what you want to hear:

- **Do you have a spouse or partner?**
  This question should come before the meeting, and the advisor should insist that any spouse or partner be part of the conversation. The decisions you will be making impact both of you. That means you both need to engage and be engaged.

- **What debts are you still paying off?** An advisor who only cares about how much money you have is not going to help you build lasting financial security. If you have $500,000 in investments but are still paying off $50,000 in student loans for your kids, $100,000 on the mortgage, and car payments, that's got to be a big consideration in your financial plan.

- **How is your health?** This impacts everything from how long your retirement income plan might need to last to whether it makes sense for you to delay Social Security. It also affects planning for out-of-pocket medical expenses that aren't covered by Medicare.

- **Do you support anyone?** A good advisor will want to understand what financial commitments you have now, or might have in the future.

- **Do you have long-term care insurance?**

- **How long do you expect to work?** If you are still working, a good advisor will want to help you run the numbers on how retiring sooner, or later, will impact your finances.

- **Do you have a trust, will, durable power of attorney for health care, advance directive, and power of attorney for finances?** A good advisor wants to make sure you have these essential documents in place.

- **When was the last time you reviewed your beneficiaries on your retirement accounts and life insurance?** A good advisor knows this should be checked annually.

Adding a pro to your team can be a smart move for many reasons. But I want to make sure you understand the terms by which I am endorsing this: You are to stay involved with your money for as long as you are able. I am not saying you must check your accounts daily, or even weekly. But open your statements every month and look them over to make sure there is nothing new or surprising. And when your advisor offers a review—whether in person or on the phone—say yes. Remember what I said? The best advisor you will ever have is staring back at you in the mirror. Make sure you stay an active part of your financial team.

At some point you may want to bring an adult child or other trusted friend or family member into the relationship. In the next chapter, I am going to sell you on the importance of having a revocable living trust. Part of having a trust is naming someone as your "successor" trustee if you ever get to a point where you can't or don't want to manage your finances. It can make sense for the successor trustee of your trust to have this role. If you are married and your spouse is your successor trustee, you may also want to include your backup trustee.

Please take your time when interviewing potential advisors. When you finish an interview, write down your first impressions. What did you like? Did anything concern you or not make sense? What about the advisor's energy? Were they thoughtful? Did they listen and really hear you, or were they more interested in talking?

If you are married, you and your spouse should make a list of pros and cons individually. Then compare your notes. It is always so interesting how we hear things differently. If you are single and have someone you trust to share your financial life with—hint: the successor trustee on your living revocable trust—you might consider asking them to be with you for the interviews so that you have someone to compare notes with.

The one question I want you to ask yourself is this: Based on your research and your conversation with the advisor, do you trust this person? Look at what you recorded as your impressions. Recount what you may have heard from referrals you spoke to. Is there anything that gives you pause?

If so, this is not the right person for you. It doesn't matter if the advisor has a great reputation. It doesn't matter who referred you to this advisor. Listen to your gut.

The most important advice I can give you is that you should never talk yourself into trusting someone. Trust yourself more than others. You know you always have your best interests at heart. Listen to your intuition. If you aren't 100% sure this person is right for you, keep looking. This is far too important a relationship to make any concessions around.

There are plenty of good advisors. You will eventually find the one who clicks. And when you do, the guidance, confidence, and calm they can bring to your retirement planning can be one of the best investments you will make.

YOUR ULTIMATE RETIREMENT CHECKLIST

❑ Seek out professional help if it will give you the confidence and calm that will allow you to enjoy your retirement.

❑ Never work with an advisor who earns commissions based on what you buy and sell.

❑ Seek out fee-only financial advisors, and confirm they operate as a *fiduciary who always puts your interests first.*

❑ Check the credentials of all candidates and run their names through the free online Broker-Check system to make sure they have not had any disciplinary run-ins.

❑ When seeking help managing your investment accounts, confirm there will be a third-party "custodian" for your money, and that low-cost index mutual funds and ETFs will be the centerpiece of your portfolio.

❑ Never hire someone you do not have 100% confidence in. Trust your gut and keep looking.

❑ Remember: You are the best financial advisor you will ever have. When you aren't sure about something, slow down and learn more. It is better to do nothing than to do something you don't understand.

CHAPTER 9

PROTECTING YOURSELF AND THOSE YOU LOVE

We are going to switch gears now. The preceding chapters have all the information you need to think through your best financial moves as you near retirement.

So now I say, *Enough with the money advice!* What I want to discuss with you next is, in my opinion, the most important work you need to tackle before you retire: protecting yourself and protecting your family. Yep, we need to have a chat about wills, estates, and all the documents that will enable your loved ones to care for you if you ever become too ill to convey your desires. In many ways, this chapter puts the ultimate in *The Ultimate Retirement Guide*.

I have to tell you, it makes me a bit nuts that many of you don't already have those documents in place.

I spend a lot of time fielding peoples' questions. Whether on my *Women & Money* podcast or at live events, I am on the receiving end of a whole lot of questions. And yet what amazes me, frankly, is that I am rarely asked about how to protect yourself as you age and how to help your family care for you if and when the time comes that you need assistance managing your finances, your medical care, and the regular day-to-day of life. Why is it that of all the questions you could ask me, you are reluctant to ask how to make sure your wishes will be quickly carried out when you die?

I think I know why. Is it because you don't want to deal head-on with anything related to getting older? You don't want to imagine yourself sick or incapacitated. Confronting your mortality is not high on your list of priorities.

I understand that these are difficult topics. I understand why we throw up defenses and conjure mental blocks and defer, defer, defer—*I'll think about it later*, you've said to yourself year after year.

Well, guess what, my friends. If you are reading this book, if you have woken up to the need to deal with retirement in a proactive way, then it already is later. That time you were deferring to? It's now.

And because you know me as a truth teller, I am going to be very direct with you. You know why you need to take care of this end-of-life stuff now? Because not preparing is a tragic blind spot that will leave you and your loved ones exposed to a lot of heartache, and potentially a financial mess. I am asking you to fight through the discomfort for the benefit of your family—and that includes you.

Who will help care for you as you age? Have you given that thought, or have you suppressed it? Either way, I am sure it's a concern that gnaws at you. That is not an emotional weight you want to carry through retirement. I can help alleviate that burden.

Have you spelled out your wishes for the level of medical care you want should you become unable to direct your own care? If you haven't, it means you may one day put those decisions in the hands of someone you haven't specifically designated for that critical role.

To not assign someone you trust—an adult child or grandchild or friend—the legal right to help you navigate your medical care and manage your finances endangers you in so many ways. I have to tell you, it isn't kind or generous to leave these decisions to your loved ones without providing them with clear, indisputable guidance.

When you do nothing, you actually do something very consequential: Your lack of planning guarantees that you and your family will struggle at a time that is already emotionally devastating. Your family may have to scramble to care for you. When you die, it leaves the door wide-open to questions about what your wishes might have been and who should get what. You and I both know those questions can lead to damaging arguments. It is so very important that a surviving spouse or life partner not have to make any big financial decisions in the year following the death of a spouse or partner. It takes time to find a new rhythm and clarity as a single person; that is not a time to be making consequential money moves. Yet if you have not arranged for a smooth transition, you may force your loved one into needing to focus on finances.

With all that on the line, I hope you will summon the warrior within, face down your discomfort, and embrace the amazing opportunity you have to create the road map that will make it as easy as possible for your wishes to be carried out—while you are alive, and once you pass.

Taking this step will deliver an immediate pay-off. You will replace all the worrying with the calm and confidence that you have a plan in place. You can relax, knowing you have taken the steps that will make it possible for you to get the support you may need at some point *immediately*, and you will have peace of mind knowing that when you pass, your financial legacy will move seamlessly to your heirs. In my experience, there is not a single person who has not felt immense relief once they got their affairs in order. I want you to experience the very same feeling, so you can get on with living!

In this chapter I will walk you through the four must-have documents that everyone needs. They are not difficult to understand, or hard to create. What may take some work, and perhaps a bit of soul searching, is deciding who you want to become your advocate along the way, if necessary, and how you want to divide your estate.

For those of you who are married, there may be some major conversations ahead if you have differing opinions on the subject of inheritance. If you have children, perhaps you need to make a decision about which child you will appoint to take the lead in your care, knowing it may set off some sibling tensions.

Avoiding these decisions and conversations does not make them go away. It will only make it worse for those who may need to step in at some point to help care for you. Besides, at this point in your life, you have navigated so much that I think you have everything it takes to figure this out.

As we age we often find ourselves thinking about our legacy. We want to be remembered for our love, our friendship, our generosity, our kindnesses. Sure, we might want to be remembered for our accomplishments too. But it is the work of our heart, not our head, that matters most.

How well you set up your family to navigate your later life will also be a part of your legacy. Will your family remember you for the mess you left behind, the arguments your silence unleashed, or will your family be forever grateful for the road map you created that gave them the ability to fulfill your wishes without guesswork? These essential documents will provide for and protect everyone. That's a powerful part of your legacy that you can ensure right now.

THE MOVES TO MAKE TO PROTECT YOURSELF AND THOSE YOU LOVE

- Create the must-have documents:

  - A living revocable trust

  - A will

  - An advance directive and durable power of attorney for health care

  - A financial power of attorney

MUST-HAVE DOCUMENT: A LIVING REVOCABLE TRUST

Okay, I bet some of you are thinking, "Whoa, I don't have so much money that I need a trust." I get that all the time. But here's the thing: A trust has nothing to do with how much money you have or don't have.

A living revocable trust is a legal document that makes it super easy for you to manage your money today, and then, if the need arises, the person you appoint can easily step in and manage your assets on your behalf.

I know many of you think all you need is a will. But let's review what I just explained: A trust helps manage your financial affairs while you are alive. A will is an important must-have document, but it only kicks into action once you die.

And if you think you don't need a trust because you have your bank and investment accounts set up as "payable upon death" (POD), that leaves you with the same problem: A POD only kicks in after you die; the person(s) you add as POD on your accounts is not authorized to use the funds or manage the funds on your behalf while you are alive.

So right off the bat we've established a reason why you need a trust.

Next, let's take a deep breath together and think about what happens when you die. If you only have a will, your family will likely need to submit the will to a probate court and get a judge's approval before any of your assets can be distributed as you have laid out. It is very difficult to navigate the probate process without a lawyer; I wouldn't recommend you even try. That means if you die with only a will, your family would need to hire a lawyer to help with the probate process. There are also fees when you go through probate. And if you value privacy, you should know that all the court filings related to your probate case are public. Anyone can read your will.

What if I told you there was a way to make sure your family will never need to deal with probate court? Once again, the answer is to have a living revocable trust. When you die and there is a trust, there is absolutely no need for anyone to obtain a court's approval to execute your wishes. The person you appointed to take over management of the trust will step in and follow all the instructions you left in the trust.

Yes, it is that easy.

Okay, now that you're on board with the value of having a living revocable trust, let's walk through how they work.

LIVING REVOCABLE TRUST BASICS

- You are in charge.

- You can spend money you place in a trust, and you have complete control over the assets you put into the trust.

- You can change your mind. As often as you want. That's what "revocable" refers to: Assets you have in a trust can be sold or moved outside the trust. You can change your plans for how you want your accounts managed if you become unable to oversee matters. And you can always change what you want to happen once you die.

The bottom line is that you aren't giving up control or flexibility with a living revocable trust. I want to repeat: You are in control of all your assets, and you retain the full rights to change the details of your trust, at any time.

When you set up a living revocable trust, you will be the trustee. If you are married, you both can be trustees. Trustee means you're in charge. You have signing authority over all the trust assets.

You will also name someone as your successor trustee. The successor trustee will step in when you die. But also, when you are alive, your successor trustee can step in should dementia, Alzheimer's, or another degenerative illness make it too difficult for you to continue handling your financial affairs.

When you create a living revocable trust, you should also make sure it includes an incapacity clause. This stipulates that if you become unable to handle your affairs, your successor trustee can step in and take control, running the trust as you directed in writing. In your trust you can also appoint someone to make the determination of when you are incapacitated. If you do this, your successor trustee (and all your loved ones) will be able to avoid a conservatorship proceeding that requires getting court approval, which will take time and money.

I want you to think about how this one document can ease some of the work ahead for your loved ones. If you have designated an adult child or someone you trust to be your successor trustee, they will not face a pile of paperwork and legal documents just to gain access to your accounts. Your family's love is unwavering. But that doesn't mean you can't take the steps today that will help ease their responsibilities at some point down the line. A living revocable trust with an incapacity clause is something you can create today to make it as easy as possible for them to help you later.

Once you have a trust, you must decide what assets to put inside the trust. This is called *funding the trust*, and it requires changing the title of ownership of that asset to the trust. Common assets that you will want to consider owning inside the trust include any real estate you own, and bank and investment accounts that are not retirement accounts.

A TRUST IS FAR BETTER THAN JOINT TENANCY WITH RIGHT OF SURVIVORSHIP

I often get resistance to having a trust from people whose main asset is a home. They tell me they don't need a trust because they have added the person they want to inherit the home to the title of the home. And they are adamant that because they own the home as joint tenants with right of survivorship (JTWROS), there will be no probate, so they are all set.

They are only partially right. It is absolutely true that owning a home as JTWROS means the home will pass to the other owner(s) when you die, without needing to go through probate. But JTWROS can create some big financial problems while you are alive. For example, if the person you add to the title declares bankruptcy, the fact that they are on the title could mean needing to sell the home to settle some debts. Or if there is an accident that the other person is responsible for, the house could become part of a settlement. In my opinion, it is best for you to keep full ownership of the home in a trust so you aren't exposed to another person's potential financial liabilities.

If you have a life insurance policy or retirement accounts with minor children as beneficiaries, I insist that you designate the trust as the beneficiary of the life insurance policy or accounts. Minor children are not allowed to inherit money directly. When you place the policy inside your trust, a successor trustee can step in immediately and make sure the guardian you have appointed (that's done in your will; we will cover this shortly) has the resources to care for your child. And rest assured: In the trust you can spell out exactly how you want that insurance used for your child's benefit.

401(K)S AND IRAS CANNOT BE OWNED BY A TRUST

Retirement accounts work by their own set of rules established by the federal government.

Each retirement account has a single owner. Even if you are married, your 401(k)s and IRAs are in your name only, or your spouse's name. For each account you are asked to designate a beneficiary. When you die, the beneficiary on record with that account becomes the owner of the account. It doesn't matter what you may have written in a trust or a will. It is that beneficiary designation on the account that rules the day.

For 401(k)s, your spouse should be designated as the primary beneficiary. If for some reason you want someone other than your spouse to be your primary beneficiary, your spouse must agree to this in writing.

If you don't name a beneficiary on a retirement account, your heirs will need to go through probate.

With IRAs, the rules are the same if you are married. If you want to name someone other than your spouse as the primary beneficiary, your spouse must sign a document that is then filed with the brokerage where you have your IRA.

So now comes a crucial question: When was the last time you checked all the beneficiaries on your retirement accounts? If you have been divorced, I sure hope you have updated all your retirement account beneficiary designations. If your ex is still listed as your beneficiary, they may get the money when you die.

Please, *please* check that your beneficiary designations are up to date.

MUST-HAVE DOCUMENT: A WILL

As fantastic as a trust is, you definitely also want to have a will. This is where you spell out who you want to pass some of your treasures to: the china set, art, collectibles. This is where you say, *Mary gets the gold necklace and bracelet, Amy gets the pearl necklace, and Rob gets Grandpa's watch.*

As a side note, it's smart to ask your kids today if there is something they are especially hoping to inherit. I think you may be surprised. Often it is not something that has the highest monetary value, but something they have a sentimental attachment to. And you may not know what that something is, so ask.

Depending on family dynamics, you might want to have those conversations separately with each child. Give each child the ability to communicate with you, rather than having to negotiate sibling dynamics.

If you discover there are items that more than one person wants, it is healthiest, in my opinion, to discuss this with everyone involved. Maybe one sibling feels more strongly, and there is something else that will please the other sibling. Having an open discussion, while you are alive, is how you prevent arguments after you die. When emotions are raw, that's the last thing anyone needs or wants.

Your will also covers any assets that you may have not gotten around to putting into your trust, and that you have not specifically mentioned in the will. When you have a trust, your will functions as a "pour-over will" where all the assets not accounted for in the trust or the will essentially pass into your trust. But there's a catch: Any assets poured into your trust must go through probate. If the size of your estate is small, probate may not involve going to court. Each state sets a limit for "small estates" that it allows to pass through probate with some simple paperwork. You can do a web search with your state's name and the term "small estate limit" to find out the rules in your state. The limits range from as little as $3,000 to $150,000. Your heirs cannot inherit real estate through this technique.

If you still have minor children, a will is essential; it is the document that assigns guardianship to your child, should both parents pass.

When you create a will, you need to name someone as the executor. The executor will be in charge of carrying out all the wishes you have included in your will, distributing your assets as you have instructed, and closing accounts. The executor will also take the lead on working with the funeral home to carry out your wishes.

You can appoint any adult your executor. Married couples typically appoint their spouse, though that is not required. If you will appoint someone other than a spouse, please be sure to ask that person if they are willing to take on the responsibility. You should never assume that someone will agree to it. They can love you deeply and yet have reservations about taking on that role.

If you have more than one child and will appoint one as the executor, I hope you will consider communicating your choice to the other children. They deserve to know. Learning this after you've passed can be unnecessarily surprising or hurtful.

I hope your family has great relationships, and that this conversation is sort of a nonevent. But for many of you, there is the potential for upset and friction. And that can feel like enough reason to avoid the conversation. I understand. And I defer to you. You know your family best. But I am asking you to push yourself just a little bit on this issue and consider the peace and harmony you can create if you tackle the conversation today.

If some of your children are upset, listen hard to what their concerns are. Maybe it is a continuation of rough sibling dynamics that you haven't been able to fix since they were children. But maybe there is a specific issue, or asset, that is at the heart of the discord. Knowing what is gnawing at your family gives you an opportunity to fine-tune your planning to address their concerns. Ultimately, you may not make everyone 100% happy. What is within your control is talking and listening today in an effort to help your family avoid friction later on. That is a part of your legacy you should be proud of.

MUST-HAVE DOCUMENT: AN ADVANCE DIRECTIVE AND DURABLE POWER OF ATTORNEY FOR HEALTH CARE

Whether you are 25 or 85, you should always be in control of your life. And one of the most personal life decisions you will ever make is how you want to navigate severe illness. I hope and pray you will always retain the ability to express your wishes directly to your doctors and your family, but that is not always how our stories unfold.

A young person can be critically injured in a car accident and placed on life support.

An elderly parent with advanced cognitive decline may be unable to comprehend a diagnosis of cancer and weigh the treatment options.

Creating an advance directive and a durable power of attorney for health care is how you retain control over what happens to you, even if you are no longer able to communicate your wishes.

An advance directive, also called a *living will*, is where you spell out your wishes to doctors (and loved ones) about how you want to handle end-of-life decisions. Do you want to be put on life support, or would you prefer to let nature take its course? If your breathing is compromised, or you have a heart attack, do you want all effort to be made to resuscitate you? If you are no longer able to eat, do you want to be fed with a feeding tube? I know these are tough scenarios to entertain, but I would venture to say that the alternative—not considering them and not having a voice in your own care—is far worse.

A durable power of attorney for health care appoints someone to speak up for you if you are unable to. This person becomes your "health care proxy," communicating your wishes on your behalf.

These documents are extreme acts of love directed at your family. With these documents in place, your wishes are clear; family members may still disagree, but you have "spoken" and your word is what matters.

I strongly recommend that once you have completed your advance directive, you discuss everything with your family. Especially your wishes regarding aggressive medical care if disease strikes at a point where dementia or Alzheimer's makes it impossible for you to manage your care.

If you were diagnosed with cancer later in life, would you want to undergo surgery? Chemotherapy and radiation? If you have a clear vision of what you want (and don't want), make that known today, because today you have the power and voice to take care of your tomorrows. That's a gift to you, and a gift to your loved ones. Making your wishes known means your children and grandchildren will not be required to guess. And having your wishes clearly known can help fend off arguments between family members who might have different end-of-life opinions. This is your life. Be clear about what you want and don't want.

MUST-HAVE DOCUMENT: A FINANCIAL POWER OF ATTORNEY

If you have a living revocable trust with an incapacity clause, your successor trustee will be able to step in and handle matters if the need arises. Still, some banks and investment firms insist that you must have appointed someone as your power of attorney for financial matters. A power of attorney for finance will also make it possible for that person to handle your retirement and pension assets that are not inside your trust. It will also be very helpful if you need someone at some point to handle all the important accounts in your life that aren't investments. Without a power of attorney document, it can be very hard for someone to wring any information from the utility company, the phone company, credit card issuers, and insurers.

Once you have created your power of attorney for finances, I want you to submit it to the institutions that handle your pension, IRAs, and 401(k)s. You want to confirm that the document meets their requirements. There is no one standard, and some institutions can be very picky. Better to know now if they have their own form they insist be used. Or in some instances, there may be additional paperwork before your power of attorney is deemed valid by that institution.

Once you have your must-have documents, you need to keep the original safe and always accessible. If anyone needs to use these documents, they must have the original.

My strong recommendation is to keep the documents in a waterproof and fireproof box that is easy to grab-and-go at a moment's notice. Evacuations for hurricanes and wildfires are becoming more and more common.

If you prefer to keep the documents in a bank safe deposit box, please make sure the name of your trust's successor trustee (and maybe even one more family member or someone you trust) is also listed on the account. If only you are named on the account, and you die (or are incapacitated), it is going to be very difficult for anyone to access these essential documents.

> **A Special Offer for Readers of *The Ultimate Retirement Guide*: Create Your Must-Have Documents for $69.**
> If you want to avoid the high fees of working with an estate planning attorney, you can create the documents you need—specific to your state's laws—by using my online Must-Have Documents Kit. I developed this program with my own personal trust attorney.
> Once you create your documents you will also receive free automatic updates. Go to suzeorman.com/retirement.

CONSIDER BRINGING SOMEONE INTO YOUR FINANCIAL LIFE TODAY

It is the rare adult in their 50s and 60s who thinks about what their energy and capabilities will be at 80 and 90. But by now you know that your ultimate retirement depends on thinking through what will be best for an older you.

And I have to tell you that bringing someone into your financial life sooner rather than later, to act as a second pair of eyes and be ready to step in and help, is a very smart move.

I absolutely understand that right now you don't need any help managing the bills and tracking your investments. But what happens if you have a stroke next week, or six months from now you find yourself dealing with a serious illness that saps your energy and makes your thinking fuzzy? And yes, I am going to go there one more time: What if at some point cognitive decline enters your life? I realize if you are married, you just assume your spouse will handle things. But what if you are the money maven in your household, and your spouse or partner isn't interested in being involved with the "money stuff"? Don't you need a backup today in the event something happens to you?

All those are reasons why the person you designate as your power of attorney for finances deserves to be brought into your financial life sooner rather than later. Because that is the person who will step in and handle things if you can't. And you will make it so much easier for them to handle things if they know all the details about your financial accounts.

I also think this person can be a great backstop as you age, keeping an extra pair of eyes on your bank and credit card statements to make sure there are no issues. If you have online accounts—and I recommend you do—this becomes easy to do.

If you don't have 100% trust in someone, it may not be practical, but I am hoping you are confident your power of attorney for finances has your back.

I also encourage you to move as much of your financial life online as you are comfortable with. Paper statements received through snail mail remain a lure for identity thieves. Nor do you want statements lying around if at some point you have in-home care. I also think it is smart to set up automated payments from your bank account for all recurring bills. Again, I know whatever system you have in place today probably works great. But I am asking you to think about the possibility that at some point you may not have the verve to stay on top of things. Automated payments are a way to build in some protection.

If you don't have children or you aren't comfortable sharing your financial life with a child—you know best who is responsible and who is not—I still hope you can turn to someone in your life who can fill this role for you, and who agrees to take on this responsibility. It can be another relative or a friend. Have a niece or nephew in their 20s or 30s? They are digital whizzes and can set you up—and handle—online bill pay and tracking your investment accounts.

If there is no one in your circle you feel comfortable asking, please consider creating a professional support team. There are services that will handle your bill payments; you can search for professionals at the American Association of Daily Money Managers (secure.aadmm.com). Vetting potential bill paying services is crucial, as there is no state or federal oversight. Asking elder law attorneys, attorneys, or financial advisors for references is smart. And then be sure to ask any potential firm for three clients you can speak with.

SPELL OUT YOUR FINAL WISHES

I also encourage you to write down—and discuss with family—your wishes for when you die. If you have a strong preference for burial or cremation, make that known. I also encourage you to be as specific as you want about funeral arrangements. If you want a fancy casket, say so. If you don't care, be extra sure to say so. Too often, nothing is said and the grieving family is left to make choices. In their vulnerable state, they may be swayed by a funeral director pitching expensive caskets and costly add-ons. If you don't want your family to overspend, put that in writing. It will make it so much easier on them. It's a gentle reminder that you always had their back. Even in death.

Are you still with me, or are you cowering under a blanket? Come on, it's not that bad. And the best part is—you only have to create these documents once. If you don't want to make changes, there's no need to revisit this topic once you've done the hard work of creating these must-haves.

In all seriousness, I understand that this chapter is not the cheeriest of topics. But taking care of these matters is the essence of love.

To know that you have done everything within your control to help your family help you if the need arises is an amazing expression of love.

To know that you have done everything within your control to make it as easy as possible for your assets and possessions to be distributed when you die is a declaration of love that will survive you.

Four documents: That is all it takes to extend this lasting and powerful expression of your love. What are you waiting for?

YOUR ULTIMATE RETIREMENT CHECKLIST

❏ Create a living revocable trust to manage your finances today and make it easy (and private) for your loved ones when you die.

❏ Use a will as a complement to a trust; it is where you spell out who will inherit your nonfinancial possessions.

❏ Spell out your wishes about medical care as you age in an advance directive and appoint someone you trust as your health care proxy.

❏ Have a power of attorney for finances drawn up; it is often required if you want someone to help you manage your bills and investments.

❏ Consider sharing your financial life with your appointed "successor trustee" sooner rather than later; it can make everyone's life easier.

❏ Spell out your final wishes.

A FEW PARTING THOUGHTS

SUZE'S STORY

A few years ago, as I was nearing 65, I went through a major life shift. I decided to end my CNBC show, which I loved so much for 13 years. I'd been on QVC for 20 years, and I didn't want to do that anymore. No one believed me when I told them that I wanted out. No one does that. At the same time, I knew it was time to end my monthly column in *O, The Oprah Magazine*. I also turned down offers for speaking engagements. I began to say no to new business ventures. I felt like I'd done everything I'd ever hoped to do in my career. I wasn't sure what my next adventure would be, but I looked forward to seeing what the nonworking future would hold for me and KT. Over the next few months, we sold our house on the West Coast and moved to a little island in the Bahamas. I disappeared from public view.

People thought I must have had a nervous breakdown.

I didn't have a breakdown, but I would be lying to you if I didn't admit that I was definitely a little bit afraid. I'd been in the public eye for so long, who would I be without a standing ovation? Who was Suze Orman if *The Suze Orman Show* no longer existed? My identity was so wrapped up in my public persona—and my happiness seemed so dependent on my professional success—that I didn't know who I'd be without all that.

Let me tell you, if you really want to find out who you are, move to an island with no shops, no cars, no theaters, no entertainment, and a poor-to-nonexistent cellular signal. That's when I decided that I was going to learn how to fish.

Fishing is the big pastime where we live. It's a recreational sport and a way to feed yourself and your family. I, Suze Orman, who used to get seasick, learned how to captain a boat. KT and I bought a Boston Whaler—a humble boat compared to the others in the marina—and started to take it out for a few hours a day. Let me tell you, from our very first hours out on the water, we thought we'd died and gone to heaven.

In the beginning, we would catch small fish, fillet them, and eat them. We were so happy, even though others were catching way bigger fish, some even four feet long. But we kept at it, because the experience of being alone, just the two of us, out on the water, surrounded by sea and sky, felt so liberating to us city dwellers. There's a saying by the writer Isak Dinesen: "The cure for anything is saltwater—tears, sweat, and the sea." It was so true for me. I felt like I was shedding layers of ego that I'd accumulated over the years. I was finally learning to love waking up and not having a plan. I loved that my calendar was totally empty. And—nothing I'd ever expected—learning how to fish made me ridiculously happy. Little by little we were learning to identify the fish we were catching, and the fish we were catching were getting bigger and bigger.

Two years into our lives on the island, KT and I entered the annual Thanksgiving wahoo fishing tournament. Wahoo are known to be one of the most difficult fish to catch. They're big—they can grow to eight feet and can weigh 150 pounds or more. They're fast and strong—they can swim up to 50 miles per hour. You need special rods, reels, weights, and lures to catch one. That is a whole learning curve in itself.

KT and I on our 32-foot Whaler with our two fishing rods were going up against experienced fishermen on million-dollar boats with crews and multiple rods. There was no way we could win, but we didn't care. It was so exciting, so invigorating, and so much fun. And, wouldn't you know it, KT and I won first place! To the amazement of everyone, ourselves included, we not only won first place for catching the most fish, but we won first place for catching the biggest fish!

The two trophies are displayed in our home for all to see. Would you believe it if I told you that I'm as proud of those two fishing trophies as I am of the two Emmys I've won?

You know what I took away from this experience?

First, by taking a step back from our busy working lives, we had the time to discover a new passion.

Second, we didn't need the biggest boat or the biggest crew to be winners. We approached the contest in the spirit of fun, and fun won the day.

Third, I realized that the joy KT and I derived from our lives had everything to do with our independence. I no longer worried about my ratings or getting the approval of TV executives. I wasn't dependent on any of that for my happiness. I was completely and totally independent. My happiness was entirely within my control.

Who would have thought that Suze Orman would be a fisherwoman, happiest spending 8 to 10 hours a day on a boat? Was that my new identity? Did it even matter? We have earned the respect of the islanders because of how we walk through this life, not because of the work we did or who we were in our previous life. I have never felt more like myself than I do right now, with everything that supposedly defined me stripped away.

The ultimate retirement is one in which you discover who you truly are and you love that person. That, my friends, is what genuine happiness is about.

Clearly, KT and I are very fortunate to be able to afford this beautiful way of life, but the lesson here is not about how wonderful our experience is. It has everything to do with the promise that awaits you in retirement. And the lesson is this: You are not defined by your work, no matter what it is or was. You are defined by who you are, how you live, and the love and respect you show to yourself and to others.

There really is life after work. The ultimate retirement is one in which you wake up and greet the sunrise each day with joy. In the ultimate retirement, you find meaning in every single day. If you make the time to look inside yourself, to marvel at the wonderment of life, you will be amazed at what you discover.

There are a few other lessons I'd like to share before you close this book.

This one's important: Patience and perseverance must prevail in the years to come.

When it comes to your money, you have to accept—and expect—that your money will have its ups and downs. No matter how carefully you plan— even if you do everything right—money, like many things in life, isn't always going to behave in predictable ways.

Sometimes you'll have more than you expect, and at other times, money will flow out and you'll have less. There may be a time when you have money in the stock market and it goes down dramatically. Or maybe you suddenly inherit a valuable piece of property. Perhaps you are retired, and then a perfect new job opportunity comes your way. I've seen this kind of thing happen with people time and time again. You think your financial life is rolling steadily along a certain track and then, all of a sudden, you're going in a different direction. I'm philosophical in these moments. This approach has helped me through my own ups and downs. When the unexpected happens, I keep my sights on the future with the firm belief that I am being taken exactly where I'm meant to go. These transitions can be exciting or scary, but they are all part of the natural cycles of life, and that includes the life of your money.

Remember always to take the long view of your financial future. If you have taken the steps presented in this book, the possible setbacks you may have today or next year or a few years from now will not keep you from loving your retirement years. Have faith in yourself. If you work hard and stay positive, you will get through anything that comes your way. That's what I call warrior mode. If you feel you have too much on your plate, here is my advice: Get a bigger plate. You can manage far more than you think. I truly believe we are never given anything we cannot handle.

Next, you must believe that everything happens for the best, that everything is a gift if you are simply willing to unwrap it. This may be the most difficult thing I've asked of you so far.

I know some of you may say, "Suze, how can it be for the best if the spouse I love so much passes before me?" "How can it be for the best if I lose some of my savings in a stock market crash?" Please understand: I am not saying such events won't be tragic and painful; I have been through some of them myself and I know how hard they can be and how much they test our faith. But I have also learned that, if we are open, they can teach us lessons about ourselves and our inner strength that we would never have learned during more comfortable times. Things that seem almost unbearable as they're happening can, in the long run, deliver spiritual riches you never imagined.

If you can believe that somehow everything happens for the best and hold firm to this belief, especially during troubled times, then you will be able to draw the good out of any situation. You will be looking for the benefit, the hidden gift, and you will be able to extract the gold from even the most challenging experiences and carry it forward. That will not only benefit you, but it will be a shining example for those closest to you.

I ask you to follow the guidelines in this book and to read and reread the parts that speak to you and your situation most directly. Internalize the advice so it becomes rooted in your thoughts, plays out in your words, and materializes into actions. Refer back to the practical guidance in these pages to verify the advice you're given from others, particularly if you consult a financial advisor. And summon the courage and the confidence that come from knowing that you have what it takes to make the decisions that are in your best interest and the best interest of the money you've worked so hard for all your life.

I want to leave you with five laws of money to carry with you into your ultimate retirement years:

Never talk yourself into trusting anyone.

Trust yourself more than you trust others.

*It is better to do nothing than
something you don't understand.*

After suffering the loss of a loved one, do nothing but keep your money safe and sound for at least one year.

If you want to find the best financial advisor, look in the mirror—for no one will care about your money more than you do.

My wish for you, my warriors, is that you never forget that with faith, integrity, and courage, everything is possible. That you know the harmony that comes from standing in your truth. That you make the most of every day of this precious life. That you live with joy and not fear.

May the love you have for yourself and for others grace everything you do.

With all my love and respect,

INDEX

online savings accounts,
173–176
certified pre-owned (CPO) cars,
41–42
charity, 26
children (adult)
discussing financial help
for grandchildren with,
24–26
discussing long-term care
with, 63
discussing must-have doc-
uments with, 268–269,
276–279
generosity to, 31
healthy money relationship
with, 13–15, 20–24
"it's only" syndrome and, 18
retirement saving *vs.* helping,
19, 41
children (minor). *see also*
grandchildren
college choice of, 40
as insurance beneficiaries,
275
cognitive impairment. *see* must-
have documents
collective investment trust (CIT),
209
college costs
college choice and, 40
of grandchildren, 25
savings plans, 40
student loans, 22–23, 40
Continuing Care Retirement
Community (CCRC), 94–97
co-signing of loans, 23–24
custodian to custodian transfer,
115, 134

D

debt. *see* loans; working years
discount brokerages, 111,
114–115. *see also* investment
strategy
dividend stocks, 186, 216–218
divorce, Social Security and, 122
downsizing of home. *see* housing

E

emergency fund
for bear-market income strategy, 148
excess savings for mortgage
payoff, 86–87
during retirement, 171–173
employment
downsizing home and, 44, 90
layoff example, 8–9
staying relevant for, 55–57
exchange-traded funds (ETF). *see
also* bonds; stocks
basics of, 210–213
expense ratio, 210, 212–213
financial advisor fees and, 243
401(k) plans and, 111
municipal bonds, 229–230
RMDs and, 184–187
executors, 278–279
expense ratio, 210, 212–213

F

family, 13–34. *see also* children;
married couples; must-have
documents; parents
adult children and financial
decisions, 13–15, 17–24
emotional decision making
about, 13, 24
generosity and, 30–32
grandchildren and financial
decisions, 13, 15–18,
24–27, 31
living with family or friends,
93, 99–102
parents and financial decisions, 16–18, 26–31
federally insured banks/credit
unions, 173–176
fees, financial advisors, 244–245,
255, 259–260
fiduciary standard, 113, 252–253
financial advisors, 237–264
assets under management
model, 242
background checks on,
249–251

Index

ABOUT THE AUTHOR

SUZE ORMAN has been called "a force in the world of personal finance" and a "one-woman financial advice powerhouse" by *USA Today*. A two-time Emmy Award–winning television host, the author of nine consecutive *New York Times* bestsellers, and one of the top motivational speakers in the world today, Orman is undeniably America's most recognized expert on personal finance.

The single most successful fundraiser in the history of PBS, Orman has received an unprecedented eight Gracie Awards, which recognize the nation's best radio, television, and cable programming by, for, and about women. Twice named to the *TIME* 100 and ranked among the World's 100 Most Powerful Women by *Forbes*, Orman was the host of *The Suze Orman Show* on CNBC for 13 years and a contributing editor to *O: The Oprah Magazine* for 16. She is currently a contributing editor to *The Costco Connection* and the host of the *Women & Money* podcast.

In 2016, Orman was appointed as the official personal-finance educator for the United States Army and Army Reserve. She also serves as a special advocate for the National Domestic Violence Hotline, bringing her message of awareness and empowerment to women who have suffered financial abuse. In recognition of her revolutionary contribution to the way Americans think about personal finance, she has received an honorary Doctor of Humane Letters degree from the University of Illinois and an honorary Doctor of Commercial Science degree from Bentley University. She has also received the National Equality Award from the Human Rights Campaign.

suzeorman.com
suzeorman.com/podcast
Facebook.com/suzeorman
Twitter: @SuzeOrmanShow